The
LIFE JUNKIE

How to become **addicted** to leading a **balanced** and **satisfying** life

SIMON A. BUBB

Arietis House Publishing

London

This is a highly rational and well thought-through book on generating balance. Its genius is not in promising happiness, but in helping you develop satisfaction – with happiness a potential (even likely) by product. Certainly, I found much to agree with in terms of both the potential outcomes and the methodology.

Robert Kelsey author of What's Stopping You? and Get Things Done.

Contents

Introduction

Thank you for choosing to read The Life Junkie.

What is this book about?

The Life Junkie describes how the Life Points system provides an objective approach to living, so that your life can be measured and improved upon over time. The Life Points system is simple: every aspect and significant things you do in your life is worth a point and, the more good things you do, the more points you get. In turn, the more points you get, you will start to feel better in life. The aim is to achieve at least 70% of the maximum points available on a regular basis.

Why was this book written?

I'd like to provide a brief history of why I originally formulated this concept to help me start living instead of existing:

1. I was not happy with my life and I didn't know exactly why.
2. I knew my life didn't have to be awful, but I didn't know exactly how to make it better.
3. Life can be made better by recognising the aspects that make it worth living.
4. Life is worth living when you achieve a balance of the various elements that make life more than just existence.
5. I realised that life can be broken down into discrete and quantifiable chunks that can be developed and scored over time.
6. By researching various theories and models of human excellence and self-development and through experiential

practice, I have devised a system which continues to work for me today.

The origins of the Life Points strategy

This book is not based wholly on my emotions or history, but on my rational ideas for a better future for myself and, ideally, readers of this book, including those around me.

These ideas have stayed with me, deep down, for many years. Throughout my 'dark years' of self-deprecation, blaming others, depression, and fear, I knew there was a truth which I was yet to uncover. That truth is that without hard work, perseverance, making positive changes, and taking action, my life would remain the same. Once this realisation, which was not a eureka moment, but a slowly rising belief which reached its peak around the time I started to read some of Ayn Rand's work, had taken hold, I was able to take control of my life and make changes. I worked through different ways to make my life better, and took inspiration from different modes of positive mental conditioning, such as CBT and NLP, to create a simple system I could use. I didn't start out with the intention to write a book about it, but as I noticed changes in my life because of my actions, it became clear that others could also benefit, and so I had to share the concept.

I have been using the 70% rule since 2011. Initially, I felt close to 0%, although actually I was closer to 20%, and simply unable to objectively assess my life because I was so lost and hopeless. It took a year before I reached the 50% mark, which I was ecstatic about because of how different (better) I felt, but I knew there was still a long way to go. I was still missing key points in underdeveloped areas of my life, such as increasing my social interaction. Since then, I have reached 70% on numerous occasions, which means my life is wonderful and satisfying on a more regular basis. My practice of self-development using the Life Points principle has shown that a reliably improved life can be achieved, even when starting from such a low point.

For whom is this book written?

This life-design system will not suit everyone and, frankly, some of you may give up before the positive effects become part of your everyday life. Some will stop because they are required to leave their comfort zone and explore new things in life. This is a natural response to change and I hope you have the resolve to fight the urge to quit. I do not wish to pressurise you into testing this system, but I will say that the results are worth the effort!

What makes this book different?

There are a plethora of self-help books out there, but you will not find many that will provide you with a step-by-step guide on how to lead a satisfying life. This book is not full of fluffy, vague ideas, but practical tried-and-tested methods in helping you live your life to the full *today*.

How will this book provide you with the steps required to lead a great life?

The Life Points system and the 70% rule are the key to success. 70% is often used as the benchmark for a higher class of success.

In UK academia, 70% grades on a degree will give you first class honours. 7 out of 10 is a good, above average score.

So if you can aim to reach 70% in your life, that means you are having an exceptional life that not many people have – while room remains for further improvement.

I realised that, if life was like a game, I could break my life down into points and see whether it improved with the more points I gained. From this simple premise, I decided to segment life into six Life Elements, which are:

- HOME
- WORK
- SELF-DEVELOPMENT
- PLEASURE
- SOCIAL
- PARTNER

If I could achieve 70% across each of these elements, then my life should become more fulfilling.

The objective is to get as many points as possible for each element, on a rolling fortnightly basis. Reaching 70% is the goal, but staying around that level and above 50% is the real end-game.

(Why fortnightly and not weekly, monthly or some other timeframe? Well, once a week would create pressure, in terms of reviewing your life so frequently. A month is quite a long time and, if improvements are required mid-month, you wouldn't know what changes to make until the following month, thus wasting precious time. You may also lose track of your progress and be unable to maintain momentum. Any longer and the idea of assessing your life and making immediate changes loses significance.)

Each element is given a weighted percentage, with all six elements totalling 100%, based on the current priorities in your life. For example, you might choose:

- HOME: 25%
- WORK: 16%
- SELF-DEVELOPMENT: 16%
- SOCIAL: 15%
- PARTNER: 14%
- PLEASURE: 14%

What benefits will you gain from reading this book?

Right now, your life is not being measured. How can I possibly know this? Well, most people haven't got a clue how to measure their lives in a rational manner: they can say whether they are happy or depressed or not, but certainly not in relation to any sort of standardised scale.

Wouldn't you like to know where you stand in your life now and how you can improve matters?

What is the overall structure of this book?

This book will take you on a journey though the six elements of life and will demonstrate how you can achieve a balance amongst them, over time. Current research, questions and answers and trial feedback will be provided, so that you can gain an understanding of how to fit these into your life.

The book draws on extensive research from the fields of neuroscience, positive psychology, psychotherapy, CBT, NLP and sociology, in addition to various other fields.

You will notice that the format of incorporating lifelong changes in your life loosely follows the 'stage of change' theory model (Prochaska and DiClemente), which theorises that the human mind cannot achieve change immediately. Rather, it experiences a series of stages before an implemented change becomes habit.

(Pre-contemplation)

Part 1 (contemplation)

Analysis of your life, % and priorities.

Part 2 (preparation)

Plan your activities.

Part 3 (action)

Undertake the activities.

Part 4 (maintenance)

Review on a bi-weekly basis.

Part 5 (relapse)

Seek assistance and support.

What's next?

The first two chapters prepare you for the journey ahead by addressing two things that you need to understand: can happiness be measured? And: what is stopping you have a great life?

From there, you move on to the main concept underpinning your new life-design: how the Life Points (also referred to as LP) principles work, and how you can implement them easily to achieve a regular Life Score (LS) of 70%. Then each of the six Life Elements (LE) is given more focus, so you can gain inspiration and ideas.

Finally, some more strategies and tools to help you on your journey towards (and staying around) a 70% Life Score.

Happy reading, and see you at 70 Life Points.

What is happiness?

Can we measure happiness and is that what we all want?

"I can't get no satisfaction."
Mick Jagger, singer with the Rolling Stones

"There are some days when I think I'm going to die from an overdose of satisfaction."
Salvador Dali

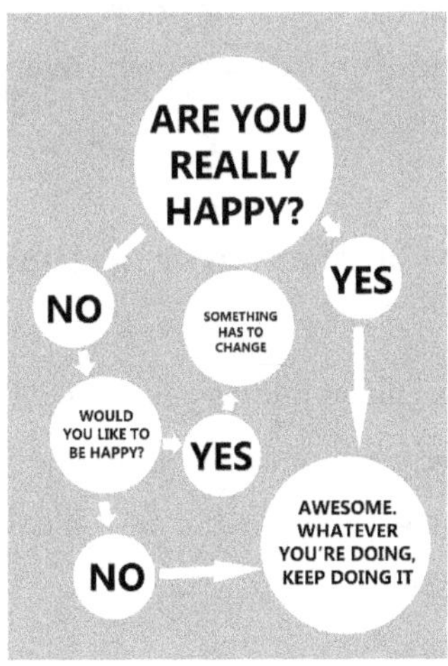

This book is based on rationality and actionable tasks, not hopes and dreams. It will give you the belief and tools to help you to step out of the shadow of your former self and become a better you.

To quote the late philosopher John Stuart Mill in his 1873 autobiography, "The best way to attain happiness is not to make happiness the direct end but to fix your mind on something else. Happiness will be the incidental by-product of pursuing another worthy goal." Or, to put it another way, as written by eminent psychotherapist and founder of logotherapy, Viktor E. Frankl in *Man's Search For Meaning*, "Happiness must happen, and the same holds for success: you have to let it happen by not caring about it". I don't agree entirely about not caring about it, but the underlying idea of not focusing on or pursuing happiness is an important message. I would say that the aim of this book is not finding happiness, but finding a balance in your life that will give you the best possible chance to be satisfied on a regular and consistent basis.

> I used to hope that my life would change for the better.
> I expected good things to happen because I felt like a good person and that I deserve it. I waited and waited but nothing changed.

Can happiness or satisfaction be measured?

I'd like to make it clear that this is not a book about how to be constantly 'happy', but about finding contentment, satisfaction, peace, and having a sense of meaning and worth in your life. As a consequence of this regular satisfaction, it is highly likely that a sense of happiness will ensue.

Your life should be about the pursuit of satisfaction rather than happiness, because happiness is fleeting and subjective. Some days you are happier than others; it varies from day to day, and hour to hour. You should be happy as often as possible, but being happy 24/7 is an impossibility. Books that proclaim otherwise are missing the point that the human brain is subject to so many variables that it is unrealistic to aim for constant happiness.

A sense of happiness can be created, to a certain extent, by taking stimulants, such as coffee or cocaine. You may feel great for a while, but that high level doesn't last for long, and you inevitably 'come down' back to your reality. If your reality is not a satisfying or pleasurable one, then coming down can lead to increased lamentation of your life circumstances – hence how many addictions start. Yes, we all want happiness in our lives, but this will come from our self-esteem and all the activities we do, and is therefore a by-product of a balanced lifestyle.

Just as with IQ, there should be HQ – 'happiness quotient', or SQ – 'satisfaction quotient'. A 'life quotient' devised by Tim Ferris in his blog based on his book *The 4 Hour Work Week*, calculates the balance between work and play. His book provides a practical strategy to minimise your time working and instead focus on living and doing the things you want to do.

You have to realise that true *contentment* and its emotional by-product, happiness, will come from the sum of the parts in your life and not just from discrete moments, which are pleasurable in one way or another, yet cannot last. Take, for example, going on flight training. This will give you an amazing buzz that is caused by the adrenalin and neurological responses in the brain; natural when undertaking new experiences, especially those that involve learning new skills and have an element of danger. After a while, the fear dissipates, your skill levels increase, and competency and familiarity will inevitably lead to automatic responses to situations that previously invoked novel sensations. Does this reduce the happiness factor and make it more of a contentment that you have achieved a successful take-off and landing? I would say so.

Contentment is subjective

This book aims to teach you how to create and build a unique reality which is diverse, rewarding, exciting, and measurable, so you know what works and what doesn't for you. You want to make your base reality as satisfying as possible. Therefore, I want to focus on peace and contentment in the context of not feeling regret for missed or missing opportunities in your life. You should feel that you have most if not all of the things you want and need in your life at this moment in time.

It is this book's job to lay down actual activities that will bring satisfaction to you in your life - to focus on real and achievable things, not purely conceptual ones. My job is to get you to go deep down to what you really think, rationally, will bring you satisfaction. Therefore, the answer to the title of this section is yes - your happiness can be measured but it's your job to measure it. No-one else can do that for you, and no-one else should have any say in what your happiness is.

When you reach 70% and are able to sustain this lifestyle, you will think about getting more and more points, but reaching 100% should not be your goal – a pursuit of perfection, which is impossible, must not become your life.

- Action not inaction is the key to satisfaction
- Contentment is subjective
- Satisfaction can be measured
- Gaining a variety of Life Points to reach a 70% Life Score is your goal

Why should I be happy?

Humans have evolved and overcome many obstacles that no other species has, and survival of the fittest and evolutionary theory tell us that we have each individually done so by beating someone else to it. We have seemingly 'won' the evolutionary race, and now, our brains have developed to a point where we can start to imagine futures with no boundaries, so that just existing is no longer enough. We are past surviving, and are now striving for all the joys and pleasures that life can offer.

Key Point

We are physiologically and psychologically predisposed to wanting homeostasis - a comfortable environment.

Darwin's theory of evolution suggests that the Human brain, evolved because of stimulation from and adaptation to many different circumstances. Significant factors which have helped us survive are arguably fear and greed. Greed is a more extreme form of feeling good about something, so much so that we want more of it, all the time. Then, once we have it, we want something else. Fear is that instinctive urge to fight, flee or freeze – to keep safe. So whether feeling good or fearful, we are physiologically and psychologically predisposed to wanting homeostasis - a comfortable environment. Comfort means safety, safety means a longer life. As we have progressed, in evolutionarily terms, this desire for comfort has reached higher levels and we now consider many previously luxurious amenities such as central heating and electricity to be standard. Using Maslow's pyramid from the *Theory of human motivation* as a guide, I believe that once our basic needs are met, satisfaction is the ultimate aim.

Following the paths we have been evolutionarily conditioned to follow is part of what leads to contentment. The brain is a complex network of interconnected pathways (neurons) which communicate with each other via electric signals and biochemistry. Pleasurable stimulation can be seen and measured in the brain by using an fMRI scanner, which highlights blood flow in pleasure centres when you are feeling good, or otherwise, about something. For example, when given reassuring statements about strongly held beliefs, the brain releases feel-good chemicals, such as endorphins, making you feel comfortable with the situation. In times of stress, cortisol and adrenalin are released raising alertness and anxiety. You can't explain why one piece of music moves you more than another, but it does; because the particular pattern of neurological pathways being excited have a more favourable reward configuration than another. As Daniel Levitin in his book *This is your brain on music* writes "Music listening enhances or changes certain neural circuits, including the density of dendritic connections in the primary auditory cortex".

Pleasing each other

For some, love is the reason for life and the only thing that makes them truly happy. For others, love is a fleeting moment that they chase throughout their lives. On a biological level, love can be described as a set of chemical reactions that take place in the mind and body to create a feeling of attachment, desire, and happiness. Love in the context of this book is explored in how it is used to enhance life, but not to rule life. A life ruled by love can often be misguided and treacherous, constantly in flux and in danger of coming apart. Love alone will not make you happy; in fact, it will make you vulnerable to exploitation and control. You will feel the need to love and/or be loved, and this can limit your potential for a balanced and rational life. But love is a great thing, that, when given and reciprocated, makes the world a better place. For self-esteem and confidence, you first need to love yourself, then others will see that and love you too.

Love can also mean passion. Being passionate about something or someone can inspire and create a positive feedback loop that will amplify your vision of the world and the possibilities therein. Love is greatest at the source.

Curiosity and exploration can only come if you are appropriately generous with your time and resources. Being generous to others doesn't necessarily mean physical goods, but I think, more importantly, is about building relationships with time and communication and support. Being generous in this way will pay dividends later on. Anyone who has ever started a business by themselves, as I have, will tell you that having a partner makes the job more enjoyable and the chance for success greater. This applies in your personal life too. You may be a solitary person but you will not be able to experience life in 'stereo' by yourself. Other people will provide information, expertise, guidance, new ideas, and love which will enrich your life.

But love is not all about 'giving'. Altruism can be bad in many ways, certainly to your wellbeing. If you are constantly helping others, it's very easy to neglect yourself, which in turn means you are not giving a full quota of yourself to others. You should be generous to yourself on a regular basis. Reward yourself with treats and experiences that enhance your world and provide an insight into the human condition.

Selfishness is an attitude to be admired. Ayn Rand in *The Virtue of Selfishness* writes, "The man who does not value himself, cannot value anything or anyone." It is a natural process which ensures our survival. If you follow a crowd and do what they do and their values are not aligned with yours, you will not find pleasure there, only frustration and resentment for not being in control. Being selfish allows you to focus on the things that make you tick, be around the people that interest you, and act according to what you are thinking. If you can't be selfish you will struggle to have a fully balanced and successful life. Many studies have shown that you can't be a people person if you are selfish, but I disagree. Being aloof, distant, and dismissive are not the hallmarks of selfishness. Selfishness means taking pride in yourself, what you are about, and what you do. You are worth what you think you are worth and no matter what others say, that is your truth and therefore the only truth.

I used to pray that my life would change and I'd win the lottery. I looked at rich people and thought "why don't you give some to us? You won't miss it. Capitalism only makes the rich richer and poor poorer". Then I read books by Ayn Rand and my attitude changed forever.

Can money buy contentment?

GDP (gross domestic product) is a universally accepted method of calculating the state of a nations' finances. However, Lord Richard Layard (professor at the London School of Economics) said that "GDP does not give a true indication of progress". In the 1970's, King Jigme Singye Wangchuck of Bhutan classified GNH (gross national happiness) into nine domains including: psychological wellbeing, cultural diversity and resilience, (based on Bhutanese people - wellbeing referring to fulfilling the conditions of a 'good life'). Money was not a focal point of the study.

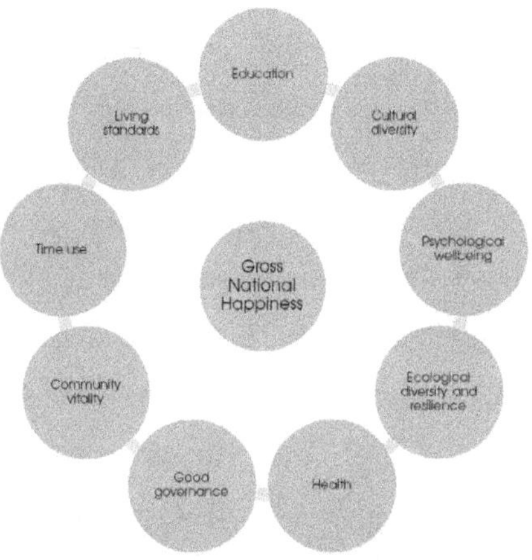

Nine domains of GNH

Money is not necessary to make you happy, as many studies have discovered. Have you ever seen beggars and homeless people on the street with genuine smiles on their faces? I have. I've wondered why, but whatever the case may be, it is possible to be content without lots of money. Of course, some would argue this is because people's expectations are much lower if they have little to no money, so simple things make them happy. The more you expect from life, the more money you need to make it happen. Therefore, is simple joy better than constant need for 'more'? No. Simple joy without trying to better ourselves and 'making do' with what we have is not a bad thing, it's just that you could, and should, do better. Once you have bettered yourself by reaching and maintaining 70% Life Points, then this level of satisfaction can be your constant.

Poverty does not preclude having a satisfying life, but it will definitely limit your life experiences. You feel the joy of waking up and perhaps spending time with family and friends, you may be in good health in both mind and body, but regardless of all these things, having disposable income opens up your world to more experiences. I get great enjoyment from travelling and seeing new places. I'm not interested in staying in hostels any more or sleeping in tents, so I will stay in the best hotel I can afford. This brings a deep sense of excitement when I see, hear, and smell new places in comfort. Buying a new car brings with it the enthusiasm which I used to get at Christmas as a child. Where I live makes me happy because I have a great view and love my area. This would not be possible if I couldn't afford the time and expense. Your attitude to money is usually the factor that changes, and with it comes a sense of freedom from the shackles of making it in the first place. Once you understand money is there to be used and enjoyed, not to be feared and worshipped, you can use it to better your life, rather than letting it control you.

Happiness is different for everyone

Your personality, genes, culture and upbringing will greatly influence what gives you satisfaction in life. You may get more joy from watching a football match live or from watching it from home. A song you like may make you smile more against the backdrop of a blue sky, whereas others prefer the night. What you need to ascertain is what things you find rewarding. What makes you tick? I'm not suggesting that you always be a pleasure seeker, as that can, if taken to its extremes, be self- destructive. But you need to know the simple things that make you happy. If you are an introvert you may take solace from being alone in your favourite armchair with some soft music in the background and time to read a book. An extrovert will find that uncomfortable and may feel the need to be around other people in an active state. Whatever your sensibilities are, this book will give you an exciting insight into the various ways you can explore finding satisfaction in places you maybe never thought of before.

Surely, no-one can be truly satisfied?

If you think no-one can be truly satisfied, then think again. Google this amusing tale: "the story of the Mexican fisherman and the American banker". You may be saying that to yourself to make yourself feel better about not being satisfied. In reality, there are many really satisfied people out there; and you'd be mistaken to think they're all millionaires.

Truly satisfied people do not have limiting beliefs. This doesn't mean they are unrealistic about what they can achieve, but it does mean that they don't believe they have limitations. They are not afraid of change or the new. They embrace challenges and appreciate what they have accomplished. Your limiting beliefs will be one of the biggest weights on your shoulders – they are that little voice in your head that says 'you're not good at that, so don't even try', or 'that project won't work, so give up'. This voice is the part of you that is trying to protect you from failure and therefore denting your confidence, but in doing so is actually causing you not to learn how to succeed. You may be bad at something, but until you try, or learn, you won't know. To succeed in the ways I have, I had to change, because my negative thought patterns were causing me to quit at the first sign of problems. My fear of failure was actually causing me to fail, until I realised the mistake I was making and turned this around to thinking about the success I wanted to achieve.

Of course, you must set yourself goals that are realistic. This doesn't mean setting low standards or going for the minimum amount of satisfaction - just don't expect miracles. If you decide that owning a yacht and your own island are the only things that will make you truly satisfied, then your expectations are too high and you are more likely to fail. You can have a satisfying life if you look at the simple things that will make you happy. Then, once those are happening on a regular basis, you can start to go for bigger and more ambitious things. Start with things that you know you will enjoy and be good at. Personally, I love driving fast, so karting and track days are great ways to get that adrenalin rush without endangering the public or my driving license! This is simple to arrange and inexpensive. A more challenging part of my life is being social. I have to make an effort to socialise because I've spent a lot of time alone and find that this is where I'm the most comfortable. However, I'm aware that I also enjoy other people's company and people who add value to my life are worth their weight in gold. Believing that I'll be a socialite and have dinner parties every week is unrealistic, yet I make an effort to meet new people whenever possible.

Will I be in control once I have a balanced life?

By following the principles in this book you will eventually reach a point where your life is the most balanced it has ever been. And you may then think: now I have reached 70%, I can stop trying. This is far from the truth. The fact is that when you reach 70% you will have learnt many new skills along the way, which will give you ultimate control over your life. The confidence you will gain from working towards reaching 70%, then actually reaching it, will be unlike anything else you've ever experienced. This is because you have made positive and real steps to live your life *now*, not simply hope for the future. This is you taking control of the moment and not letting the good parts of life pass you by. When you can effectively reach 70% on a regular basis, the control and freedom you have in your life will surpass the dreams of generations before us and people in less developed or less free countries. You will have not only been given the gift of life but also the gift of freedom.

Summary

- Leading a consistently satisfying life is your goal.
- Happiness is a by-product of being satisfied.
- Whatever gives you satisfaction in life is your choice.
- You can achieve a successful and fulfilling life as long as you are prepared for change.

Exercise

Make a note of six things that you can think of which would make your life satisfying.

Visit 70lifepoints.com to receive guidance and support on Chapter 1.

Your journey has now started, but what is stopping you from continuing?

What is stopping you from having a great life?

Do you have any barriers, both perceived and actual, which may be stopping you from living your life to the full?

"Our doubts are traitors and make us lose the good we oft might win, by fearing to attempt."

William Shakespeare

A rational approach to life is not easy. You are surrounded by the comfortable and subjective views of the world and your society. Irrationality and limiting beliefs pervade any society that is based on altruism and the good of the masses, rather than on the individual. Remaining in your comfort zone, will ultimately halt your progress towards leading a great life.

This book is not based on one specific philosophy, but on the virtues of life itself. One could argue that objectivism, a philosophy developed by Ayn Rand, is at the heart of this book. It has, to some degree, influenced the underpinning conjecture that, without a rational outlook in life, you will be controlled by whim and emotion, and as Ayn Rand put it in her book *The New intellectuals*, "Man has the choice to think or evade". However, objectivism does not provide a practical guide to living one's life.

In a similar vein, in Jamie Smarts book *Clarity*, he does not provide a practical guide to living, as he believes that a 'steps' process is an 'application' not an 'implication' and therefore needs to be learnt and implemented. To a certain extent I agree with his premise that clarity comes from inside-out thinking, but once you have that clarity, there is no guide as to what is next.

Self-discipline will help you attain your Life Points, but being consistent in positive actions will eventually become second nature. Without discipline, drive and motivation, your results will vary greatly and your goals will take longer to achieve, if at all. Discipline will allow you to add actions, layer-by-layer, until your life has a natural flow to it that doesn't require extra effort to maintain. Once you are in the flow and you realise you're in control of your thoughts, this level of clarity in your life will allow you build an even better lifestyle.

Time is precious and will not come back to you. Using the Life Points strategy outlined in this book will change your life and you won't waste more time wondering why your life feels unsatisfying.

> I used to think that self-discipline implied obsession, frugality and boredom. In fact, the more time I spent doing the things I wanted, being self-disciplined was actually fun.

Many ideas in this book have been inspired by my experience, research and observations, with a variety of subjects such as NLP (neuro-linguistic programming), CBT (cognitive behavioural therapy), psychology, meditation, mindfulness and hypnotherapy. Shakespeare wrote "to be or not to be'", while Dr Peck of *The Road Less Travelled and Beyond* fame wrote "to think or not to think". This notion does not automatically relate to reasoning: just because I think, doesn't mean I am rational by default.

Ms Esther Duflo, an economist at MIT and co-author of *Poor Economics*, evaluated the effects of being very poor, using a programme developed in Bangladesh. Ms Duflo aimed to ascertain participants' thoughts pertaining to hope and self-improvement and claims that they did not believe they could get out of their penury, due to the fact that they were constantly thinking about how to survive and were struggling day-to-day. Duflo found that, when participants were more optimistic, they started to save more and had hope for a better future. She also discovered that the poor had 'poor thoughts', which kept them in poor areas and poor living conditions. When hope increased, work productivity increased, depression levels decreased and participants worked 28% longer.

Positive thinking alone is not enough in changing your life; you have to take *action*.

- Rational thinking will help you gain Life Points
- Limiting beliefs are irrational and a result of conditioning and circumstances
- Self-discipline is the first step towards enriching your life
- Positive thinking and positive actions are the key to a great life

Money is not the root of all evil

You cannot escape the influence of money. Much like your body metabolism at rest still uses calories, even if you stayed in one place, you would still spend money. This is an integral aspect of a capitalistic society. Capitalism has not had good press in recent years. The economic uncertainty we face today has been attributed to the greed, irresponsibility and 'wilful blindness' (As Margaret Heffernan describes in her book *Wilful Blindness*) of the financial leaders in many western countries. Is capitalism solely to blame for all the financial woes many are facing today? No: rather, capitalism has given you a platform from which to use the rules of supply and demand to create wealth for yourself. Socialism and communism failed as models of freedom for the people. You are free to read this book because of capitalism and I'm free to write this book because of capitalism. You probably want more money and, by being balanced, you will attract money and thus be able to spend more money. This is an advantage for bettering yourself.

How you think about money will play a significant part in your ability to attain it and spend it.

I remember growing up in a poor household. Not totally poor in monetary terms, because we had some of the usual creature comforts, such as TV, video player, video games, toys and so on. What was definitely poor was the attitude to money. My parents would usually buy the cheapest version of everything and expenses where constantly budgeted. This way of living stayed with me pretty much until recent years. I've grown more sophisticated and am able to avoid buying cheap (and often buying twice), but the 'poor' mentality, although in remission, still remains in one form or another.

> ## Key Point
>
> Capitalism has given you a platform from which to use the rules of supply and demand to create wealth for yourself.

Spending money used to be difficult for me. I felt uncomfortable spending money and wouldn't treat myself by buying an expensive or 'up market' product. Until I grew to appreciate money for what it is, a commodity to enjoy, I was unable to spend. Once I learnt to spend money, I made more of it. I'd like to say that it's some cosmic dance or law of attraction that has ensured I'm attracted to money so it is attracted to me, but I simply became more accustomed to letting money in and out, which has improved the quality of my life massively.

You may be reading this book and thinking that you have no chance of achieving a 70% Life Score without lots of money. You'd be wrong: you *can* achieve this without having a great deal of money, but I believe you will need a reasonable amount to lead a fully satisfying life. After all, holidays aren't free and neither is dining out. Thus, you will require a certain level of income to have a better chance of reaching 70%, but this isn't essential. What *is* essential is that you appreciate money and are able to use it without prejudice. You should not squander your cash and should save some, but, ultimately, you must spend it on your life, if you are to enhance your Life Score. Your LS is the most important thing in this. Money will certainly help with some activities, but many require only time and effort, without a big financial outlay. Once you are free from feeling trapped by money, or a lack of it, you will be free to explore your world, calm in the knowledge that you are in control and are not being controlled by money. Money will not make you happy, but it will help

> If you embrace things you know nothing about, your world view will also expand and will bring variety into your life that you never thought possible. I recently went to a workshop entitled 'Orgasmic Meditation'. I had no idea what to expect and was initially sceptical and quite nervous, but the experience proved to be one worth having.

Why am I so afraid?

To be afraid of failure or rejection is normal. It isn't a comfortable feeling and we would all rather live without it. In fact, experiencing failure and rejection is how we learn to improve. If everything went our way, we would not be as smart as we are. Failure means that you have tried, and it is the trying that is vital: failing to do so means that you are missing out on the opportunity to succeed and to learn. As Robert Kelsey describes in his book *What's stopping you?* you are potentially either a person with 'High AM' (achievement motivation) or 'High FF' (fear of failure). Being afraid of failure may prevent you from doing something, but I can guarantee that you will regret not giving something a go. This can be as simple as not talking a woman or man you found very attractive, but were afraid to approach, for fear of rejection. I know this has applied to me on numerous occasions. This same feeling of discomfort, when you can't predict the outcome, is stopping you from enjoying life and will prevent you from achieving a 70% Life Score. Having a balanced life involves doing things you've never done before or don't feel particularly good at. The aim isn't to become the best at everything, but to acknowledge what you are god at and what you can improve upon.

How can life success be achieved if I'm depressed?

Being depressed is an obstacle to overcome, just like any other. Granted, it is a rather big obstacle, but something that can be overcome nevertheless. Having been depressed on a number of occasions, I understand how debilitating depression can be. One of the biggest factors for me was a sense of overwhelming failure and a feeling that I could never be happy. When I first became depressed, I knew that I needed to address the problem, but was unable and unwilling to seek help: I just wanted to curl up and die. Reading this book would not have helped, because I was not ready to change. I knew something was wrong and that I couldn't survive in that state in the long term, but I couldn't be proactive without acknowledging my weaknesses. If this book helps you to come out of a depression and on the road to an amazing life, I will be extremely proud to have helped you. However, it may be that you need to seek therapy and begin your road of healing before you start to address the principles in this book. This is because this book in itself is a road of discovery, for which you will need to be focused and ready for change.

CBT modelling

At the beginning of this book, I proposed that happiness, or, more specifically, satisfaction, can be measured if we take the time to objectify our lives in as logical a manner as possible. Many would argue that you can't measure life, yet professional psychologists say they can measure depression: if one side of our psyche can be measured, then why not the other? Therapies are there to try and gauge how much sadness is in our lives and how we are deal with that. Psychoanalysis, positive psychology, CBT, CAT, DBT, NLP, hypnotherapy and a whole host of other therapies exist, many of which aim to understand your thinking patterns and restore your thought processes to what is considered a healthy norm. On a personal note, a combination of medication, CBT, mindfulness and NLP worked wonders for me. I had initially tried just medication and counselling, but felt that simply talking about my problems was causing negative thoughts to increase, rather than diminish. CBT and, to a slightly lesser degree, NLP helped me understand the reasons why I was thinking about certain things and gave me an alternative perspective on my life. This was invaluable, as one of things I found when I was depressed was that I was deeply alone and that no-one understood me and therefore couldn't help me. I thought that my brain chemistry was wrong or that my neurons weren't wired properly. There might be some truth to these claims, but what is definitely true is that, with effort and practice, you can train your 'plastic brain' (as Norman Doidge explains in his book *The brain that changes itself*) to think differently. There is a therapy that works for you.

Why should my life be great if it has never been that way?

If you continue to do the same things you always have done, your life will remain the same. If you are not happy with your life, then change is the only way to success. It seems so simple to say but, in practice, is harder than most people think. You may be unhappy and dissatisfied, but at least you are comfortable because you can predict each day. You are afraid of change: why? Do you think you might make things worse, or fail? Your future is not yet a reality and the choices you make today will affect how your life pans out. By making positive changes to your life today, you will stand a much higher chance of achieving a fulfilling life. At the end of your life, do you want to look back and realise that you didn't enjoy life? I didn't think so! Change is universal: the universe is expanding, the human race is evolving and yet we still try to resist change. You must embrace change and realise that you need to make changes to your life, if you are to achieve a 70% Life Score. Even if you think your life is great right now, it is useful to know what is working for you, how to ensure it stays that way and how it can be improved upon. Without change you will remain the same and be left behind, while others around you have fun.

> **IF YOU WANT SOMETHING YOU'VE NEVER HAD**
> **YOU MUST DO SOMETHING YOU'VE NEVER DONE**
> **:-)**

The truth is that many people in the world are enjoying their lives right now. They have balance, security, excitement, love and experience in their life, in addition to many of the other things we associate with a fulfilling life. They may have read this book and started their journey to a 70% Life Score already. Some may have achieved a fulfilling life without reading this book, while others were simply lucky enough to be born into the right environment or culture and already have all the things you will gain in reading this book. The point is that attaining a 70% Life Score can be done: I achieved it and continue to hit that mark. Not every month but I improve each year. If I can do it, then so can you! You might never before have experienced a sense of elation for no apparent reason at a random time of day, but it can and will happen, as the human mind is fully capable of this. I often wondered why some people smiled at me in the street. I thought they were high, or listening to something funny, or just plain weird. Now, I too have times when I notice myself smiling in the street, and I laugh a little inside.

Ditch the resentment

If you are not happy with your life and blame others, you will find it hard to find a solution to your dilemma. Even following the rules in this book to the letter won't help you when things don't go your way and you blame others or your past for things not going to plan. The fact is, others have done you wrong and you have wronged others. Move on and don't let people you believe to have hurt you continue to do so indirectly. Just because one person hurt you in the past, it does not mean that all people will hurt you, or that you are going to be hurt again because of that person in your past. Playing the blame game distracts you from your real aim in life, which is to enjoy it consistently, ethically and fully. I used to blame my parents for everything bad in my life, from my depression to my poor record in holding down relationships with women and friends, my perceived lack of social skills and even the fact that I did not make enough money. Everything was explained away by saying 'well I had a crap upbringing, so it's their fault my life sucks'. There is a certain amount of comfort in blaming others, in that it takes responsibility away from yourself.

This may seem extremely simplistic, but think about this scenario for one moment. If you could go back in time and replace every bad experience or feeling with a good one, how would you be today? Different, better, happy, the same? The point is, the less time you spend being negative means the more chance you have of being at least neutral and at best positive. Being negative wastes time and energy. When things are not going well, all you do is worry about it. You may have nightmares, stop doing things that you enjoy and spend more time dwelling on the bad. You go around aimlessly, not quite knowing why you are doing things: this is a massive drain on your resources. When you are in a good place, good things come naturally to you. It's a bit like when you have a poor posture. The body uses more energy to maintain a good posture, whereas, if you already practice a good posture, the body uses less energy in maintaining it. It may seem bizarre, but many people love to be negative. They get a sense of comfort in thinking that everything is bad and that nothing good will happen. This is defeatist and a sign of weakness. You should always be aware of the downside to life, but aim to remain positive.

People drag

If people in your social group are actively holding you back and you have valid evidence to support this view, then you have to take the harsh view that these people should not be in your life. By holding you back, I mean discouraging you from trying new things, not helping you when you ask for advice, not trying new experiences with you, being negative and so on. They may add value in other areas, but are not congruent with underpinning your life goal, which is to be successful and satisfied. These people may even be part of your family; regardless of who they are or how long you've known them, if they are not with you, they are against you. Your life is more important to you than theirs is to them. You must take some tough decisions, with the first ensuring that you only have people in your life who add value to it and support you. Negativity will slow you down and limit your chances of success. You might think that this is being aloof, selfish, or distant, but I say what is wrong with being that way? You might have outgrown your current social set and need to move on. Your new life will bring you into contact with people more akin to you and you will feel better for flushing out the undesirables

A positive world

In much of the western world and other places around the world, your life expectancy now is higher than what it was just 100 years ago. This is a massive advantage, in that you can enjoy your lives in relative safety. You no longer have to scrimp and save just so you can enjoy retirement at the expense of enjoying your youth. Your ability to exert your will to change your life is given to you by the democratic and capitalistic nations. This is a great gift because, although there is much competition in every aspect of life, you are given a clean slate to make of it what you wish. You may have to start later because you didn't have the experience to make things happen at a younger age, but this does not mean you cannot be successful at any age.

Even in the richer nations of the world, you will have to work smarter and harder than the people around you to get noticed. You will have to compete on many different levels if you want to have a satisfying life. To get a partner that you want will require you to offer something that others can't and you may have to fight for them. To get by in your career, you will have to impress your managers and play the game of office politics. The resources available, in terms of teaching you how to succeed, are immense. Just by reading this book, you have taken a step towards improving your life for the better. You can attend seminars and workshops, getting support in all areas of life, from addictions and business advice, to psychotherapy and counselling, many of which may be free.

The opportunities to reach a 70% Life Score are so much greater than you realise. Yes it will be a challenge and reaching 70% will take time and effort, but the tools required to help you achieve it are in this book and out there. There is no need to feel stifled by a lack of resources. Look and you will find, ask and you will receive the answer.

It is strange to think that you might be your own worst enemy, but it's probably true. Yes there are still gender, racial and other biases which may influence your choices and of those around you. However, *you* are much more likely to sabotage your life than any external force. Without positive affirmations in your life, you may tend to lean towards a negative outlook, which then turns inwards to self-deprecation and lower self-esteem. It's a common fact that the mind filters out the world to suit your state of mind and will thus notice positive things if you are in a good mood and vice-versa if you're in a bad mood. The most likely reason you are not where you want to be is within you. Typically, the fear of success can be just as potent as the fear of failure, either of which acts as a barrier to success. You may be afraid that you will never be happy and that trying is futile, or that you might be happy temporarily but this is unlikely to last, so what's the point in getting there in the first place? Fear must be conquered, if you are to achieve a 70% LS. Fear will cause you to doubt your values, motives and actions and will deter you from experimenting and learning from life experiences. Put simply, you cannot let fear take over your life.

Summary

- Your past does not have to dictate your future.
- Blaming others and not taking responsibility for your life not being satisfying is a waste of time.
- Being rational will help you overcome limiting beliefs.
- You will have a great life if you believe in yourself.

Exercise

Make a note of six things you think are stopping you from having a satisfying life.

> Visit 70lifepoints.com to receive guidance and support on Chapter 2.

You know that you can and will have a satisfying life. Now let the fun begin.

3

The 70% Life Points Rule

Now you understand what happiness is, it's time to understand the practical Life Points strategy that can measure your satisfaction

"Life is really simple, but we insist on making it complicated."

Confucius

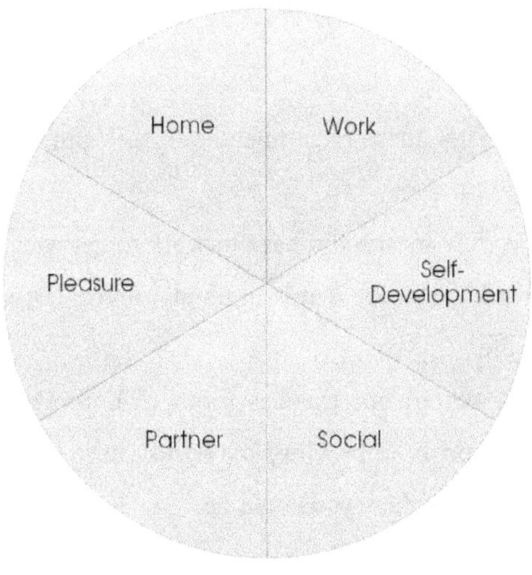

The six Life Elements of a satisfying life

Your life experience is made up of six Life Elements, which are (in no particular order):

- HOME
- WORK
- SELF-DEVELOPMENT
- PLEASURE
- SOCIAL
- PARTNER

The aim is to get as many points as possible for each element, on a rolling fortnightly basis. You get points for things you do in each element. Reaching an overall score of 70% is the aim, but regularly staying around 70% is the real end-game.

Life points strategy

From the combined scores of your elements, you can find out your Life Score. Here's a rough guide to how the numbers translate to satisfaction in your life.

- Below 20% and I recommend you seek professional help to get you on track.
- Below 50% means you have to work to get your life on track. You will feel a lot is missing and you are not satisfied with your life.
- 50% is better, but there is room to improve. You can tell your mood is improving, but lacks that clarity and feeling that you are where you could be.

- 60% means you're on your way to reaching 70%, and you will feel positive and the beginnings of satisfaction in your life.
- 70% feels great and you have reached your goal. Life automatically feels satisfying on a consistent basis, and you are keen to stay here.
- 100% is perfect (don't expect this – perfection is impossible – but you can aspire towards it!)

The 70% rule

Your aim is not perfection, but to reach 70% for every two weeks. Every two weeks you will add up the points from the previous two weeks.

Under the points system you will be following, these are the standards to remember.

- Each element is given a weighted percentage equalling 100%, based on the current priorities in your life.
- Your biggest priority can get no more than 25%, the 2nd priority no more than 20%, and the rest no less than 10%.
- Your 1st priority is the one element that, if at or close to top marks, gives you a stable platform from which to build the other parts. This Life Element should be gaining you a relatively easy haul of regular Life Points.
- The 2nd priority again ties in with providing confidence, a means to grow and develop the other parts. These two elements will be your 'bases' or 'foundations'. A way to think of these is that if you had nothing but these two things sorted, you could still have a comfortable and productive, albeit imbalanced existence.

My home is my biggest life element at 25%, and the next biggest is social at 17%. Work used to be my 2nd biggest priority but in the past year I have given this less focus (even though I still work very hard and enjoy it on occasion!), and realised that I was being more social and this was positively affecting my life, more so than work.

Therefore, I decreased the importance of work and increased my social maximum.

Your top two Life Elements might be partner and social: you don't put your home above all else in terms of giving you a sense of security or confidence. You could just as easily live in a box just as long as you have a social group and a partner.

Or you might have self-improvement and pleasure as your two base Life Elements. Work for you is not as important, and you have the opportunity to focus on develop your mind and body, and gain all the various entertaining and pleasurable activities.

Here were my percentages:

Life Element	Start of writing book	End of writing book	Reasons
Home	25%	25%	I felt that I was only truly going to be able to free myself and build a better future if I was satisfied with where I live

Work	20%	15%	Work gives me a sense of purpose and satisfaction (when things go right!) and challenges me in ways nothing else can. Money earned gives me more options to live the lifestyle I want. More recently, as making money is less in focus, I've decreased the points allocated here.
Self-development	16%	16%	I'm always trying to learn something new, or improve what I already have and keep my mind and body healthy. Otherwise I would get bored very quickly. Through self-development I gained knowledge and skills which empowered me to change my life.
Pleasure	14%	14%	Although I love doing things that give me pleasure, trying to get 25% in this area every two weeks would be exhausting! Hence why it's not my priority, but I still want to make sure I take time out to enjoy myself

Partner	13%	13%	I'm comfortable by myself, however, my preference is to be in a long term relationship, and I will make an effort to make this happen.
Social	12%	17%	This is an area I have improved upon and become more used to. I see the major benefits it has had on my life, hence why it now has more Life Points allocated.

Note that, as you change over the years, your priorities may change. Once you have chosen your Life Elements, keep them the same for about six months, then review if necessary.

In recent months I have been more sociable than I've ever been, and have therefore changed that %. Work is also becoming less of a priority, so I have lowered my corresponding % accordingly.

Let's get you started

You will notice that the format below loosely follows the 'stage of change' theory model which theorises that the human mind can't just change straight away, but goes through a series of stages before one can say a new change has become a habit.

We can pass the pre-contemplation stage though, where you were not even thinking about change. You are above this level because you're reading this book.

Part 1 (contemplation)
Analysis of your life, %, and priorities

Part 2 (preparation) Planning your activities

Part 3 (action)
Doing the activities

Part 4 (maintenance)
Reviewing on bi-weekly basis

Part 5 (relapse)
Seek assistance and support

Part 1 (contemplation)

You are now aware of the six L i f e Elements, and the first step is to prioritise them.

> ### Key point
>
> Remember that ALL the Life Elements are vital, just that number six is not the most important in giving you a stable base. You want to focus on other areas of your life so you can start to build on the other life elements when you feel mentally strong and confident.

With this in mind, start to think about which elements are more important to you *right now* and list them from 1 to 6, 1 being most important.

If you are struggling to prioritise, one way to figure this is out is to use a mental exercise to go to extremes; pick one element and think about whether you could live without it in comparison to another element. Work your way through each element this way until you sort your elements.

Here is a table for you to put in your first thoughts about life points. It's OK if these change as you read the book. Once you have finished the book you will then decide on what you think is the right balance to start with.

Life Element	Life points %	Reasons
1.		
2.		
3.		
4.		
5.		
6.		

To help you understand how you can allocate % for each Life Element I will provide an example from Jane.

Jane has decided on these as her top six:

1.   Social

2.   Partner

3.   Pleasure

4.   Work

5.   Home

6.   Self-development

Examples: Jane

Jane has a steady career since leaving university a few years ago. She has lots of friends, is close to her family and is not especially ambitious. Jane currently lives in a cramped and low quality house share in a cheap part of town and is dating one of her fellow lodgers.

I will suggest a % for each element for Jane in the next sections, which may help you decide on yours. Remember that this is *your* journey, and therefore there is no right or wrong way to allocate the percentages. However, you will know when you have found the right balance when you start counting your points (Part 4).

Allocating percentages

Now you have your six elements prioritised you can allocate a maximum number of % (interchangeable with the word 'points' or 'Life Points') for each.

HOME

To decide on the amount of points the home element should have, think about what you expect from your home and the quality of life it can offer.

Points can be given for any number of aspects such as:

1.   View
2.   Furnishings
3.   Space
4.   Size

5.   Cleanliness

6.   Interior design

7.   Neighbours

8.   Local demographic

9.   Area

10. Location

11. Brightness

12. Lighting

13. Smell

14. Comfort

15. Warm

16. Close to shops

17. Transport links

18. Parking

19. Technology

20. Mod cons

21. Acoustics

22. Communication reception/broadband/phone

23. Safe

24. Makes you feel special

25. Value for money

At the moment, where I live is regularly giving me about 22-23 out of 25 points. There is no need to keep tallying up the points for your home each unless there have been recent significant changes which would regularly increase/decrease your points. Where I live now misses out on size (it's only a small apartment), and a few minor annoyances.

In essence, my home is providing me with most of the things that I could ever want from a living space *right now*. Of course I would like to upgrade at some point but my home is a great base this time and I'm very satisfied with it.

The things you value from your home will be different but use the same methodology of scoring it. If you give your home only 10%, decide on 10 things you want from it (not what it currently offers). In this case, your home is not your top priority, so even if you get 10% you might not be totally satisfied with it but it is adequate for your wants and needs right now.

Example: Jane

Jane chose 14% for the home element. She would eventually like to move somewhere nicer but is not bothered at the moment. As long as she is safe, relatively comfortable and surrounded by her friends she is fine with her current arrangement.

WORK

Whatever you spend most of your mental and physical energy doing during working hours can be considered work in that context. If you are a student then work is researching, attending lectures, and completing assignments etc., or a part time job. If you are retired then work might mean looking after grandchildren, and attending the garden. For the unemployed, looking for work by attending workshops, going for interviews, posting CVs, applying online, this is work but cannot be fully classed as work as an end in itself. So work means a task orientated activity that has a definitive purpose and is rewarded in some way.

How do you score points for this?

You cannot think about what is your fantasy job (mine would be formula one driver, rally driver, or astronaut!). You have to think about your work and whether it is meeting your current and future aspirations and what its highest realistic points can be. You may be in a job that even at its best is not going to get top marks. This is a sign that you should be looking for something else.

As I'm sure you've gathered already, being 100% objective is virtually impossible when allocating percentages, but think about certain positive parts of your job which will help you score it:

1.   Interaction with others (clients, suppliers etc.)
2.   Satisfaction from completing tasks
3.   Financial reward
4.   Challenges
5.   Enjoyment
6.   Variety of tasks
7.   Teamwork
8.   Management (your manager and you managing others)
9.   Staff interaction
10. Delegation
11. Meetings
12. Business development
13. Location
14. Hours (do you have enough time to focus on other elements?)
15. Flexibility
16. Freedom
17. Achievements
18. Recognition

19.   Reputation

20.   Networking

On bad weeks I've been down to about 8 points and the best has given me about 16 points (this occurred when I had split my week between various projects which kept my mind stimulated). Recently I've been overwhelmed with more repetitive and one-sided work which has put me around 10 points. How I've scored this is a combination of intuition and rational scoring rather than solely counting attributes such as those above. This makes me think that as I'm finding it hard to get consistently high points that I may need a change to my work or lower the points and allocate them elsewhere (especially if I'm maxing points in another element).

As with home, your work Life Element won't need each Life Point counted each week if it remains relatively stable. If you have a job which changes regularly then you would have to note these changes and score them accordingly.

Example: Jane

Jane likes her work but she is not currently motivated by money or career so work gets 14%. Jane's keen to move up the career ladder in a few years. She thinks she will score reasonably well on this element but is a bit bored with work and would rather allocate more points elsewhere.

SELF-DEVELOPMENT

This is defined as any task which requires a certain degree of mental concentration, learning, physical effort or application of skill to effectively overcome specific obstacles and challenges. It is different to work (but you may also get self-development points at work) as you get points for each self-development activity rather than how work is in general.

Is sport a pleasure or self-improvement point?

It can be self-improvement and pleasure depending on the activity. There may be the pleasure from winning or the participation, but in most cases it will be part of self-development because you are doing something which challenges your body and mind.

This element is pretty easy to score. There are a large number of activities which could count towards your self-development points:

1. Reading
2. Writing
3. Exercising
4. Taking a class (e.g. life drawing)
5. Learning something new
6. Therapy (CBT, NLP etc.)
7. Sport
8. Hypnosis self/hypnosis
9. Being creative (making music, drawing, designing)
10. Attending lectures/seminars
11. Meditation
12. Yoga
13. Trying something new

14.   Improving aspects of your physical and mental self (eyesight correction, lipo, counselling)
15.   Reviewing your Life Points every two weeks
16.   Experimentation
17.   Practicing skills

Note that if you partake in the same activity multiple times throughout the week e.g. you go to the gym three times, you will not get 3 points but just 1 for the two week period. The key is to have variety.

Example: Jane

Jane is not reading much at the moment, and is not sporty or particularly creative. She gives self-development 11% as she has recently finished university and feels like 'switching off' for a while and therefore developing herself is important but not top priority. She sometimes prefers meditating at home to going out socialising.

PARTNER

This element refers to anyone in your life with whom intimacy is present or is a mutually desired outcome. If you have a platonic friend (regardless of gender) then they will give you mainly social points and other points, but not partner points.

When you spend time with your partner doing different activities you will get a point. For example, you live with your partner and three times a week you go out and do various things such as dining out, theatre, and walk in the park. That's 3 partner points, plus points for the activities themselves e.g. 1 pleasure point for dining out, 1 for theatre etc. If you live with your partner and you see them every day but you are always indoors just watching TV, then only 1 point is awarded. Many other activities also count. For example, let's say you have a really good, stimulating conversation then this is a point (remember that if you converse every day you still only get one point, unless the conversation is wide-ranging and varied). You go on holiday together, you give each other massages, go hiking in the mountains. Whatever the activity is, you should be doing as many different things with your partner as possible.

If your partner is your top priority (they should not be offended if they are not) and you've given the maximum of 25% then you have a lot of things to do every two weeks to reach top points!

If you don't have a 'steady' partner and you are dating, then the same points rules applies. However, I wouldn't advise going on twenty dates with twenty different people just to get 20 points.

You'll be pleased to know that sex is also counted as pleasure points!

Example: Jane

Jane is very much into her boyfriend whom she has been dating for about a year and enjoys spending time with him and doing lots of different activities together. She gives the partner life element 20%.

SOCIAL

Your social 'sphere' includes anyone you interact and engage with on a social level who is not your partner. Work related conversation with a colleague at work is not a social point. However, chatting to that same person over lunch without discussing work related topics is a social point. Talking to that same person over and over again does not give you more points. You only get points for each unique person and unique way you socially engage with each week. Remember the key is variety; are you really being social if you only speak to one person on a regular basis?

I specify engage because it's easy to interact with a stranger, but harder to engage through conversation and body language.

A phone call is a point. Even a reasonably long text message conversation is a point. However, a short message conversation such as the one below, is not:

Hi, how r u? ☺

I'm great thanks

Cool. We should meet up soon. Yep how about next Wednesday. Nice, let's do it!

Example: Jane

Jane enjoys being around people and feels less comfortable being alone. She has lots of different friends and engages with them regularly each week. She doesn't think that any of the other areas are more important than her social sphere and will have enough activities to be able to get close to maximum so the social element gets 25%.

PLEASURE

My definition of pleasure is any experience that excites one or more of our senses more so than the norm of any average moment in the day. It is tangible and repeatable. It can also be something that if done too often can become addictive and dominate ones thoughts and actions. It can be something that makes us smile (inside or outside) or feel a sense of well-being. From a physiological and neurological perspective it is something that excites the pleasure centres of the brain, or the 'reward circuits'.

Needless to say I am referring to rational pleasures that create no conflict with others or bring harm to others. What is an irrational pleasure? Harming yourself or others while giving you 'pleasure' is irrational and immoral.

I do not intend to list all the different pleasures that any one person can possibly experience is one's lifetime. Suffice to say you must remain in control of the temptations to over indulge in certain pleasures, and be able to choose as and when you participate.

Any time you have had a pleasurable experience which is a discrete moment in time and repeatable, give yourself a point. You do not get more than 2 points per week for doing the same thing over again so variety is important. E.g. you eat at a restaurant three times per week, which is a pleasurable experience for you, you still only get a maximum of 4 points over the two weeks.

You may have sex five times a week (good for you!), but unless you are doing something different so the experience is varied each time then you still only get 2 points per week. Limiting points encourages you to have variety in your life and not become dependent on only a few activities that you repeat regularly.

Example: Jane

Jane spends a lot of time with her friends and boyfriend and they are always in or out doing fun things. She gives the pleasure element 16%.

Part 2 (preparation)

OK so you have prioritised your Life Element and allocated maximum % for each.

Now, for each element list all the things which could give you points in each using my guide above. Be as objective as possible but don't be too prescriptive. Add things which you may not have thought of before and would like to try. It should not be easy to get to 70% but give yourself a chance to get there and beyond.

Chapters 4 through to 9 will give you more ideas on where you can get points from.

Part 3 (action)

Get a diary or wall mounted calendar to write your events on. I put it on my phone and wall calendar to not only remind me of what's coming up but to keep a record of what has happened, or not. Each Sunday I try to plan my week ahead and book in one or two events and meetings with friends.

You can also use various websites to help you with ideas for things to do.

Read chapter 10 for more ideas on how to keep your points coming in regularly.

Participate in as many activities and experiences as you can.

Part 4 (maintenance)

Reviewing your Life Points.

There are some guidelines to remember about gaining Life Points.

Guide	Examples
Points that come from self-destructive behaviour should be avoided.	Bad addictions such as drug abuse, alcoholism and so forth
Prioritise gaining points from activities which have longer term values over quick fixes	Although immediate points are great and you should definitely do them; mix these activities with events which take longer to complete. For example, if one evening, you have a choice of going to a comedy show with your partner which will give you an immediate pleasure and partner point, or going to a class where you can learn something new over a number of weeks; choose the latter (and invite your partner!)
Choose activities which will give you more points per activity.	You have a choice of going to a seminar where all you expect is one self- development point, or a social gathering where you expect to make one pleasure and five social points; choose the latter. Although don't pressure yourself into getting points if you don't want to. See point below.
Trying to get points for the sake of getting points is not recommended.	If you don't feel like doing something, then there is no need to force yourself. Although I suggest you come out of your comfort zone to explore the world, make sure you enjoy it too.

Give yourself no more than 2 points per week for any given moment for the same activity (for Social, Pleasure and Partner). For Home, Work and Self-development, only give a maximum of 1 point per activity/aspect.	You eat at a restaurant four times per week, each of which was pleasurable. You only get 2 points per week for this. You have sex 3 times per week, again you only get 2 points per week (unless you spice things up and it's different each time!). If you socialise with the same group of friends in the same way e.g. going for drinks each week, then you get a maximum of 2 points per person you interact with. If you do other activities with them such as going on holidays, theatre etc. then you gain extra points. If you read every day and go to the gym three times per week you would get 2 self-development LP (1 LP for reading and 1 LP for the gym) for the two week period.
If the overall outcome of the experience is neutral/negative give yourself 0 points.	For example, you attend a lecture which was not enjoyable or informative, so you don't get the 1 self-development point.
There is no rush. Be patient.	Over time, gaining LP and keeping track of your LS will become second nature.

I combine tallying my points with a self-led CBT type session every two weeks, but you can just count your points if you wish. It usually takes no more than five minutes to add them up.

Chapter 10 provides more details on how to structure a review session. You can use the Life Points excel spreadsheet provided on the 70lifepoints.com website to help you keep track of points.

Below is an example of how Jane has scored her last two weeks:

Social 25%	Partner 20%	Pleasure 16%	Work 14%	Home 14%	Self-develop ment 11%	Total Life Score
23	11	13	6	6	5	64%

How did she calculate these points? Let's analyse them. Remember that the aim is to be as objective as possible but there will undoubtedly be some subjective scoring taking place. The way you score yourself will be different to someone else but if you are being honest, your LP and LS will be as accurate as you can make it.

Social: She lives with four other people and interacts with most of them every day. As she can only get a maximum of 2 LP per week per type of interaction (she didn't go out with any of them; just chatted at home) she gets 16 LP (2 LP per housemate per week for two weeks). She spoke with her brother on the phone once (1 LP), went out with her two best friends (who don't live with her) twice (4 LP), and went to after work drinks once where she socialised with two colleagues (2 LP) - she doesn't usually speak on a personal level with colleagues during work hours.

Partner: Jane's boyfriend stayed over a three nights each week for two weeks. On those nights, they went out somewhere different each time; cinema, dinner, nightclub etc. (6 LP). They spoke on the phone twice each week (4 LP). They gave each other massages once (1 LP).

Pleasure: Massage (1 LP), six nights out with her boyfriend (6 LP), drinks with best friends (2 LP), sex five times over two weeks (4 LP).

Work: Harder to quantify but Jane gave points for hours; she only works 9-5pm and no weekends. Freedom; no need to take work home or do more hours than necessary. Location; the commute to work is short and gives her the courage to occasionally cycle there in the summer. Satisfaction from tasks; her work is not too challenging but she gets a sense of satisfaction on completing tasks and also gains recognition from her colleagues and line manager. Financial reward; Jane's current job is not a huge earner but provides enough to live on with plenty spare to enjoy.

Home: This LE doesn't fluctuate in LP very much. Jane quite likes where she lives but the house is old and bit decrepit. She gave LP for: close to transport links and shops, safety, value for money, communication technology such as wifi, and nice neighbours and lodgers.

Self-development: Jane gave LP for: One mindfulness session, one Life Points review, one massage (good practice and learning more each time), went to a play where she learnt something new, and reading a book a few times each week.

Jane's opinion of her LS: A great couple of weeks. A variety of activities with lots of fun things going on. Work is not especially interesting and she would like to live somewhere better but it will do for now.

My opinion: Jane is doing very well. She's not that far from reaching 70% and is aware of some areas she can improve in future. Although I think she has placed too much pressure on herself and her partner to achieve 20%. They already spend quite a lot of time together participating in a range of activities and would need to spend even more time together being more adventurous to reach 20%. I suggest she drops the partner % a little, and adds % to *pleasure* and *self-development*, a Life Element in which Jane has much scope for improvement.

Part 5 (relapse)

Keeping a record of your Life Score is a great way to keep track of your life and will eventually become second nature, much like a diary. But there will be times when life becomes overwhelming and you either forget to keep track or don't try to get points at all. In this case you should not feel like you're alone but use the professionals at 70lifepoints.com for guidance and support.

At the 70lifepoints.com resources page you can download a graph of my life over the previous two years. You will notice the graph has peaks and troughs although the trend has been slowly climbing upwards. Expecting highs and lows is normal and over time you will know why you are not scoring highly and how to increase your Life Score.

This system continues to work for me. It has given me a sense of well-being and satisfaction that I never had before. I'm fully aware of which areas I need to improve upon and when things aren't going so well I can see exactly what's not working.

This system requires 100% belief in yourself and 100% honesty to yourself. If you don't have these yet then the system will eventually make you believe.

It is not easy and is not supposed to be easy. Having a great life takes time and effort.

Summary

- Life consists of six Life Elements.
- Your aim is to get as many Life Points in each element as possible.
- Reaching a 70% Life Score is where your life will feel satisfying.
- You get points for things you do in each element.
- Keeping a record of your progress will help you reach 70%.
- Persevere and you will get there.

Exercise

Think about and write down what percentages you would give your six Life Elements.

> Visit 70lifepoints.com to see an example of how I count my Life Points to tally my Life Score.

Let's get you started with getting towards 70%.

Element One: Self-development

Why continuing to learn is the key to keeping your mind and body healthy throughout your lifetime

"No matter who you are, no matter what you did, no matter where you've come from, you can always change, become a better version of yourself."

Madonna

BE A BETTER YOU+

Self-development is a term to describe activities which enable you to learn and grow as a person. This can be physical things like going to the gym, mental stimulation such as learning a new language, or emotional exploration using meditation or forms of therapy.

What makes us the superior life form on this planet is our ability to think. There are animals that are physically superior to us in many ways; stronger, faster, able to fly, breathe underwater, and change colour. But our ability to rationalise the world around us, learn and implement new skills as a species, and manipulate our environment is [currently] our power alone. It seems we are designed to progress towards an unknown and limitless future, as demonstrated by our desire to be better versions of ourselves. Even the laziest of us might look in the mirror and think: 'I'd like a flatter stomach', or 'I wish I were smarter', desiring improvement of the mind and body. Self- development revolves around activities that facilitate learning, growth, and physical, mental, and emotional well-being.

Key attributes of self-development include taking part in activities which you are passionate about and interested in, and also exploring new experiences. You will find it a lot easier to keep the self-development element scoring well if you choose activities that you enjoy. Think about any things that you have put off doing before. List them in order of how easy it would be to get started.

Some things you are passionate about or interested in learning more about can be really simple to get started. For example, I find drawing a very relaxing activity, which helps take my mind away from any stresses to focus on the moment. You don't need much to get that started, just a pencil and some paper. There are likely to be life drawing classes on your area, and if not, just draw what's around you.

If you are anything like me, during any given day I will think of things that can be improved in what I see around me. I notice every little thing which appears less than perfect or out of place and think about ways to fix them. More often than not I leave them be, but occasionally I attempt some DIY and change things around. Self-development can be a great excuse to become more practical and useful at different things. Or it can improve the skills you already have. Learning new skills that are useful in your everyday life will make your life better and, in many cases, easier. Other useful self-development ideas include keeping fit; your everyday tasks will become much easier as you get stronger and fitter. The idea is for you to become, as William Glasser describes in his book *Positive Addiction*, positively addicted to activities which improve your life.

Your self-esteem and self-worth will be greatly enhanced when you follow a regular pattern of engaging with self-development activities. You will feel a sense of achievement with each one of these activities because you will learn something, you will challenge yourself, and you will be out of your comfort zone as you increase your knowledge and skill set.

Every time I finish my workout at the gym, I have a great sense of accomplishment. I enjoy the process, but mostly enjoy the buzz at the end! Not all activities are like that, of course. When I go to a fascinating seminar and I find the content engaging, then the journey is the reward. Booking things in your diary isn't enough. You need to attend as many events as you can to ensure you are getting a balanced and interesting week. You will feel empowered, because you've chosen to go to the events and (ideally) will have gained what you wanted from them. Being active and progressive with your knowledge, skills, and attributes means that you are not spending time on useless and shallow exploits which don't add to your life score.

A dream of mine is to gain a PPL (private pilot's licence), but in the past I have put it off because I was too busy and it takes time and concentration. I've now set my sights on achieving this goal and have started clocking up flying hours.

Scoring your self-development

For every activity you do that involves learning something, improving your physical, mental or emotional self, doing something creative, sporty, or healthy, give yourself a point. Examples include:

- Training courses
- Self-hypnosis
- Reading regularly/every day
- Attending a gym/exercising
- Playing a sport regularly
- Learning new skills e.g. music classes, sport coaching
- Being creative: art, music, writing, photography
- Attending lectures/meetings that inform/revitalise your mind/spirit
- Meditation
- Mindfulness
- Improving your mental ability
- Improving your physical attributes
- Emotional balancing

How to unleash potential

Your potential is tied up with how you see yourself and any limiting beliefs you may hold. These inner beliefs are very personal to you and may or may not be true. But the pre-existing truth is irrelevant, because whatever you believe to be true, is true. Sounds too simple to work, but the fact is that you can become a different person overnight if you are willing to believe it. Improving yourself in all aspects of your life is part of reaching 70% and staying there. If you think you don't need to learn anymore, you're wrong – and you'll be sliding backwards before you know it. The best thing you can say is that you know you know nothing. That means you will always be searching for more useful information. As your knowledge grows, so does your ability to improve various aspects of your life. Your mental state will improve through NLP and CBT, your physical state will improve through exercise and sport, your intelligence will improve through reading, learning and seminars, and your emotional state will improve through new insights, mindfulness and so on.

Key Point

The more things you try, the more chance you have that something will go right for you. Open your mind to the possibility that positive thoughts will lead to positive outcomes, and it is going to happen.

The success or failure of your self-development will depend on your willingness and ability to be open. This does not mean succumbing to any whim or desire which side-tracks you from your goals. It means being open to the possibility that you will have an amazing life, and that you are able to learn and grow within your lifetime, and give inspiration to others. Being open requires you to remain closed to negative values, people, and limiting beliefs. Being open asks that you treat yourself with respect and be honest about your strengths and weaknesses. You must be open to the fact that you might not achieve everything you've ever wanted, but if you focus on key areas, and keep trying, you are much more likely to achieve many great things in your life. If I told you that out of ten things you've always wanted to achieve in your life, you would get seven, wouldn't you consider that a success? I would. Even getting just one of those things means that you have something or done something you've always wanted.

Why are challenges important?

If you don't push the boundaries of what you think you can achieve, how do you know your true abilities, your true potential? You'll never know if you don't try. Just imagine, one day when you are old and most of your life is behind you; would you want to think that you didn't try things or push yourself? I know I wouldn't. You must be aware of self-development and how important it is to be a better you. You may think you're okay now, but you can always strive to be better. It doesn't have to be a relentless pursuit for perfection, as this is an unattainable goal. But by pushing your capabilities to the maximum and stepping out of your comfort zone whenever you can, you will find your life takes on a new, higher definition, whereby you are more aware of your existence than before. Each thing you do will bring more and more satisfaction to your life because you'll be challenging yourself on a regular basis. Challenge the status quo, even if things are great. Duplicate the things that work and eradicate those that don't.

As often as possible, surprise yourself, by which I mean participate in activities that you wouldn't usually do and which challenge your typical behaviour and thought processes. For example, I went to a workshop based on the practice of 'orgasmic meditation', or 'OM'. It was a workshop which gave the participants the opportunity to voice their innermost thoughts and feelings about themselves and others. I had never heard people speak so frankly about their sexuality, and I honestly felt a bit uncomfortable, yet it was interesting to hear others' fantasies, and I laughed inwardly (and sometimes let out a giggle) when certain things were said. I learned a little more about myself, and, by being out of my comfort zone, also gained some confidence in being able to attend a similar event again and not be embarrassed. Participate in activities which no-one would believe you would do, e.g. meet a group of strangers and talk for a couple of hours about random subjects.

Many people suffer from low self-esteem and this condition manifests itself in many ways. In behavioural terms, low self-esteem will limit your life choices to those you feel comfortable with and which have less chance of failure. This is playing it safe, to maintain however much self-esteem you have. By taking small risks and trying new ways of doing things to enhance and improve your life, you will undoubtedly get things wrong. However, the more things you try, the more you will find that work for you, and from these you will build your self-esteem. Try to bring your social group to your new activities, to provide further support. Then any failures will be shared, and you will build on those and not get disheartened. Set yourself goals and targets, e.g. learn a new skill every two months. Each skill learned will give you the energy and confidence to succeed at the next skill.

Experiment with life

You only live once, so I think it makes perfect sense to experiment. Experiments don't have to be scientific, or accurate, but you will see from your Life Points that certain things will work better for you than others. This is what I mean by experimenting. Your life can be a blank canvas upon which you paint your desires and dreams. There will always be some limitations, but you should put these thoughts to one side and add things into your life *right now*. By doing something different *today*, you are saying to yourself and the world around you that you are in control and you want to have a satisfying life, not under the influence of others. By trying new things and learning new skills, you are announcing your entry into a new world which is fun, exciting, and full of wonder and surprise. Not the old world of fear, failure, and low self-esteem. This is your chance to shine, so don't waste it.

By trying new things, you are likely to become a more interesting person. Have you ever had a conversation with someone who hadn't done anything new in years? I have, and it's painful to listen to. You will hear nothing but regrets, fantasies that will never materialise, excuses as to why they are not successful, and a general lack of self-belief. This is a waste of life. If the human race hadn't tried new things, we would still be swinging from the trees. The brave few who dared to explore new ways of doing things are the ancestors to the innovators and adventurers (such as yourselves) of today. They grasped that doing the same thing over and over again and expecting things to change or improve is insanity (as Einstein wisely said), and therefore experimented with new things.

If you think your lifestyle does not warrant you the opportunity to become an innovator with your own life, then you need to seriously analyse what is stopping you. Perhaps a significant change of lifestyle, thoughts, and behaviour is necessary to bring a more open nature to your life. You will not reach 70% if you stick to doing the same things. In fact, you are rewarded for doing new things by receiving more Life Points. This book is about changing your lifestyle to a point where the resemblance to your former self would be difficult to ascertain.

It is a challenge to keep up to 70%, but then that is the point of life; to strive to make it worth living and exciting on a weekly basis.

I am a very different person to who I was even a mere two years ago. Yes, many traits will never go away, but my lifestyle has changed dramatically and for the better. It took much practice and changing of behaviour, but eventually it becomes second nature and one no longer has to work hard at achieving it.

Fitting activities into life

It's important to build up layers of activities, so that you always have a grounding of things happening that bring a foundation of points with little planning, e.g. you might go to the gym three times per week, and this is counted as one of your self-improvement points. You might play a sport once per week. So these two activities become your 'base', and provide you with two self-improvement points. Another example might be dinner once per week with friends, which gives you social points and pleasure points. These base points can be things that are based at home, however, I suggest, whenever possible, having some base activities that have to be done outside, requiring effort, whether mental or physical, to attend.

Home-based regular activities can include reading non-fiction every day, meditating and performing self-hypnosis (which I use as a way to reinforce positive affirmations), or NLP. From a set of base activities you can start to add further things that add value to your life. It will be a case of trial and error to find out which activities go well with others. Time and money constraints will affect which activities get done; however, your goal should not be compromised. Also, do not chase things which negate or take away from your base activities. If you have an extra event, this should fit around what you already do, e.g. you have a dinner date at 7pm when you would normally go to the gym. In this case, you should go to the gym earlier to accommodate the dinner date.

In all cases, your aim is to make sure each activity can be enjoyed to its fullest, and if you think they won't, then rearrange.

Finding time

What is taking up your time? Can you add any activities inside these, your commute to work is 1 hour each way. During this time you could:

- Learn a new language
- Read a non-fiction book (perhaps this one!)
- Plan your week ahead/plan how to reach your 70%
- Practice NLP

What if you work long hours and come home exhausted (even though you've filled your one hour commute with useful stuff)? Well, there will be certain days in the week when you do not wish to partake in any extra activities, regardless of how much you value them. For example, this week I had a massage on Monday night, went to a philosophical debate on Wednesday, produced music in a studio on Friday, and played badminton on Saturday. If you think this would be tiresome to you (which is not the aim of the system), you'll find that once you start, your energy levels will improve as will your passion for life. However, you will have to acknowledge that your lifestyle and attitude towards your time has to change in order to reach higher levels of life satisfaction.

People's energy levels are finite, and, depending on a number of factors, will vary from day-to-day and between individuals. You have to calculate what you are *actually* capable of achieving at any moment in time and work towards achieving that. If your energy levels, both mental and physical, will be a limiting factor in achieving your goals, then this needs to be addressed before attempting to reach 70%. If you try to reach 70% with no mental or physical energy, then you are doomed to failure. But part of what brings you to 70% are activities that bring your energy levels up, such as self-hypnosis, meditation, mindfulness for mental energy, and exercise, sport, and a better diet for physical energy. If you are balancing elements well, you will be increasing your supply of energy as the demand grows.

What is well-being?

Well-being as a term is broad. As an industry, it is big business. It spans various aspects, including the body, mind, nutrition, and the 'spiritual'.

Combining physical exercise with mental clarity and purification is an ideal use of time. Yoga is a fantastic activity to help with both physical fitness (although I recommend cardio-vascular and weights for all-round fitness) and achieving some mental fitness too, both stretching and relaxing at once. I have to admit that I've injured my shoulder doing yoga and find stretching quite a challenge, but for many it's the only way they exercise, and I would never argue with a yoggie! Your physical and mental wellbeing are the supporting base from which you will grow as a person, and giving yoga a try covers all the bases. You can practice yoga at home, using either yoga videos online or music to help.

Jon Kabat-Zinn has a brilliant selection of meditation and mindfulness audio recordings which I'm sure you will find useful if you spend time practising with them. I was introduced to Dr Kabat-Zinn through group mindfulness sessions, which were parts of my therapy to overcome depression. Part of this was also CBT (cognitive behavioural therapy), the logical thought processes of which I found a great partner to mindfulness. Meditation and mindfulness give your brain the chance to release and open up to new ideas and thoughts, without the pressure of being productive or efficient. Meditation gives you a chance to reflect and think about how you are doing in life.

Slowing down in this way will give you the energy to keep going full steam ahead without breaking down. Making your mind still will pay dividends in your everyday life. I meditate once a week for about twenty minutes, then have a longer session once a month using an audio track from Dr Kabat-Zinn as guidance. I find this gives my brain a chance to offload old thoughts which are clogging up my more useful thoughts and potentially holding me back.

The two kinds of self-development

There are two major forms of self-development: mental (which can also include emotional) and physical. So let's take these one at a time (though, as with all things, there will be overlap).

Mental self-development:

Without knowledge, you won't know how to move forward in your life. You have to keep your mind active and open. Increasing your knowledge gives you a much better chance to take control of your life and improve it. People who keep their heads in the sand are not willing to change and will be stuck in a loop, going nowhere. You must be a person who sees change not only as inevitable, but to be as important as life itself. If you are not changing, you are going backwards, as the world moves on around you.

Isn't the brain unchangeable in adulthood?

The brain is not hardwired for life. With practice and dedication, you can change your brain to create a better version of you. You are unlikely to suddenly become a mathematical genius if you weren't one already, but you can reach beyond what you thought you were capable of and achieve many great things, if you just allow your brain to adapt. Changing your brain may sound like science fiction, but changing the way you think about something is changing your brain, and various techniques allow it.

For an example of how simple a thing changing your brain is: I never used to like parma ham. I didn't hate it, but I would avoid it whenever it was offered on a menu. As I got older, I didn't have such an aversion to it, and now I enjoy it on occasion. The same goes for medium-cooked steak; I never used to be able to stand any semblance of blood in the meat and always had it cooked very well done. I now prefer the meat medium. These may seem like trivial things, but it takes a change in thinking to accept new things in your life. Your brain is designed to filter out things you feel are hazards, even if those things are not truly hazards.

The brain can be trained, just like the muscles in your body. The more exercise it gets, the better it becomes at dealing with those tasks. As Jim Lawless wrote in his book *Taming Tigers*, "dealing with fear and discomfort is a learned skill". If your usual working day doesn't involve challenging your brain or coming out of your comfort zone, then find things you can do during it that will. Spend your breaks doing puzzles. Sudoku is a classic, but if that's not your style, then there are many other ways to challenge your mind.

Reading is another great way to get your mind working. It causes you to use your imagination and expand your horizons, getting you out of the small-world mentality you may have. Reading the right publication will give you insights into the world that you would never have otherwise. Books, magazines, ebooks, etc. are the best way to get started with learning, with minimal fuss or financial expense. This book was written so you can see how your life can be amazing if you just take the time to look after yourself, and to give a practical strategy for making that happen. Just reading this book will have a positive effect on you, called 'bibliotherapy'.

If reading is not your thing, then you can watch documentaries, learning new things about the world and the universe. Take part in things you've never done before and you'll be amazed at how quickly you can adapt.

Even at my age, I enjoy video games. My favourite types are first person shooters and driving simulators. I've found that over the years, they have provided much entertainment, frustration, and excitement. I don't recommend you rely solely on simulated environments to engage your brain, but there is no doubt that games can exercise your hand-to-eye coordination, solution finding strategies, engaging survival instincts, and other positive rewards. In fact, some video games are specifically designed to be mentally challenging; see Portal, Antichamber, Spacechem, and others in this genre.

Why should I go to seminars?

Seminars are a great way to learn more about subjects which fascinate you without committing to long periods of study. Many seminars are free and typically range from an hour to a few days. Even subjects that you think are well beyond your scope of understanding become less intimidating when you attend a seminar, because of the usually informal nature of them. I find science very interesting, but many of the theories are bewildering. Just thinking about taking a course in astrophysics seems like a stupid idea, as I would be well out of my depth, but attending a short two hour seminar about celestial phenomena is much more accessible. Don't be afraid to go to events that are in fields outside your current realm of understanding, because you'll be surprised how much you pick up.

Another great reason to attend seminars is that you are likely to meet people with similar interests and characters to you. They have also taken the time to find the seminar and attend, so they obviously have some similarities to your way of thinking. This gives you a chance to engage with new people and network, and perhaps make friends. You must be open to the idea of socialising beforehand, otherwise it's quite easy to attend a seminar then leave without ever having spoken to anyone. I like to make it a goal (when I'm in the mood) to speak to at least two people per seminar, and, if appropriate, gather contact details for further communication. The atmosphere is likely to be comforting, because you know the subject interests you already; therefore, try to lower your guard and be open to new encounters.

Going to a seminar can be a catalyst for gaining ideas about many different aspects of your life. For example, going to a 'Millionaire Mindset Intensive' seminar gave me the idea to separate my bank accounts for different uses. Going to a Gerry Roberts book seminar gave me inspiration to help me complete this book. Every event I go to I try to learn something from, and even if it's not useful to me at that time, I pass on information to friends I think will find it useful. It needn't be business-orientated – ideas can help you gain a better understanding of your life and how to make it more interesting. You may get a design idea from seeing a decorated stage, helping enhance the look of your home. Someone may mention something that gives you an idea for a holiday. The possibilities are endless. You don't have to be a genius and come up with totally new ideas all the time. Feed off other people and tweak their ideas for yourself.

Tony Robbins and other motivational speakers have user-friendly approaches that encourage you to explore your thoughts in a safe environment. More confrontational seminar approaches exist, with past examples mesmerisingly described in Luke Rhinehart's book, *The Book of Est*.

Courses and classes contribute to self-development

For many of us, just getting out of the house is a challenge, especially in the winter months, which in the UK seem to last for most of the year! Attending classes and seminars gets you out and about, doing something interesting. The main differences between classes and seminars are probably the more active nature of classes, and the longer-term commitment involved – but they can also pay great dividends beyond those of seminars.

Every month or so, I go to a drop-in life drawing class in the evening. I have found that this is one of the most effective ways to combat stress and get over a difficult working day. There is nothing like being creative to stop all extraneous and negative thoughts from entering your consciousness and affecting your mood. Life drawing, for me, is a learning process; each time I get slightly better, and I find new ways to draw. The models are always different, so I can't get bored easily.

Look at websites such as these below to find suitable courses and classes for you, some specialising in certain industries such as health and fitness:

- www.beabetteryoucourses.co.uk
- www.meetup.com
- www.schooloflife.co.uk
- www.eventbrite.com

There are classes and courses all the time, every day, every week, so there is sure to be something suitable for you.

Having a class to go to will create a sense of excitement and may add that extra bit of incentive to have a great day. That's why it's vital you choose activities you will find stimulating and a wide variety so you don't get bored. These classes may also be enjoyable, offer the opportunity to socialise, and teach you something, so you are likely to get a few LP for each element the class enters into. For example, when I go to life drawing, I learn, which gains 1 self-development LP, and usually have a chat with other artists, which gains a few social points. Be excited about your classes, because you can be sure that many people are too lazy to get off their butts to do anything new, yet you are exploring the world and enjoying it to the best of your ability. Your positive attitude will transcend the activity and enter all aspects of your life.

Furthermore, many of the skills you use in your classes will be transferable to everyday life. For example, taking cooking lessons has taught me patience and not to force expectations on myself to learn too quickly. Going sailing has taught me the benefits of teamwork and morale. Taking flying lessons has taught me about paying attention to details and remaining calm under pressure. Many of these character attributes I had already, but these different classes have helped me consolidate them and put them into practice.

Taking a course is an act of intent. The intention is to learn, because you admit you don't know everything you want to, and that you wish to know as much about things which interest you as possible. By admitting this, you are being open and honest about your limitations but not trapped by them. Pushing the boundaries on what you think you can achieve will help you towards a successful and balanced life in future. Learning and using new skills is the key to self-development and should never stop.

Is it harder to study from home?

You no longer have to attend a physical class to get the benefits of the learning experience. As more and more people take up studying from home, the advancement of distance learning has matched demand. E-learning has come a long way, and is now a sophisticated method of study without many of the usual barriers, such as lack of time, money, or students' inability to travel. The Distance Education Academy (www.distance-education-academy.com) is a popular site where you can browse hundreds of different courses to start at any time and complete in your own time. Although e-learning requires a suitable device with an internet connection, the technological knowhow required to use the software is very low, and anyone can start learning with minimum fuss. I suggest choosing one course at a time and setting yourself a time target to complete it.

Many courses have videos to support your learning. Videos can often be interactive, but even if they're not, they will provide an added level of mental stimulation over just reading. Videos are a great way to learn – and almost certainly more useful than watching TV. Keep your workbook open and make notes at any points of interest in the video. If necessary, watch the videos repeatedly until you understand the underlying concepts.

Set aside some time every week for your studies and you will eventually complete them. Time management is key to getting your coursework and assessments completed (See chapter 10 for time management strategies). Use the recommended learning hours as an indication on how much time you need to dedicate to the course, although you may be able to complete it sooner.

If non-interactive learning materials are not your style, yet you still wish to study at home, then many course providers offer a live tutor/webinar/mentor feature. This will give you the chance to ask questions and gain a response almost immediately. Webinars are a way for you to feel 'connected' with your training provider. When a topic is explained in a live format, you may find that you are learning more rapidly, because you know that it is live and therefore won't get repeated (unless the session is recorded and available for repeated playback). If the tutor's face is visible, it may be comforting for those who require some 'face-to-face' contact and reassurance. Furthermore, the course you have chosen may be delivered in a different country altogether, so live streaming can be the only way to meet or speak to your tutor.

> ### Key point
>
> If your emotional and mental health are in need of retraining and balancing, consider some form of therapy, such as CBT and mindfulness.

What types of therapy help?

I went untreated for intermittent depression and negative thought patterns for many years. I kept my emotions hidden and my feelings muted. I didn't discuss them with anyone, yet felt I needed someone to help me. After I had built up the courage and admitted I had a problem, I went for counselling. This didn't work for me, but it led to CBT and medication, which got me back on track.

Self-hypnosis allows you to enter a state of relaxation where positive and self-affirming statements can be more easily assimilated into your subconscious. You can do self-hypnosis any time of the day, but I suggest later in the evening, when you can relax without distracting thoughts such as work taking hold. You can use a script which, once learnt, can be repeated over and over again until you know it off by heart, but I suggest using an audio track from a professional to assist you in getting into a deep, trancelike state of relaxation. Using self-hypnosis has helped me on many occasions when my energy and enthusiasm waned. These 'waves' of highs and lows in terms of motivation are normal, but can be smoothed out if I use self-hypnosis to help me focus.

There are many websites that provide wide-ranging libraries of audio from professionals. I tend to use self- hypnosis for things like work motivation, willpower, self-esteem boosters, and so on.

Cognitive behavioural therapy is the practice of analysing negative thought patterns and behaviour, and logically devising a strategy to stop those negative thoughts, which in turn will allow positive actions and behaviour. The process in itself can be very effective, but as I found out through personal experience, during the initial sessions, it was more beneficial when used in conjunction with medication (for depression). Once the depression was cured and medication ceased, I found that CBT helped me on a regular basis to keep track of my thoughts. Every two weeks, I conduct CBT on myself using the techniques I learnt from therapists and reading books. Although it is not as thorough or robust as sessions taken by a professional, I find it gives me a valuable insight into any issues which are starting to develop and helps me combat them before they get out of control. CBT really helped turn my life around, and I recommend you see a CBT professional (even if you think you are in a good place), because you can always learn about how certain thought patterns may be limiting your potential.

CBT is a form of therapy which aims to provide solutions to problems. Psychoanalysis is more of an underlying search for the mental characteristics of a person without necessarily providing practical solutions. Therefore, for many, psychoanalysis is simply a way to understand their minds better; childhood grievances may be unearthed, for example. Understanding the root of these thoughts may open your eyes to why you react in certain ways in certain situations, which may in turn give you solace. I prefer to have information which can be used in practical ways, but there is nothing wrong with being more aware of how your mind works and therefore becoming more likely to know when things aren't quite right.

What is NLP?

NLP is Neuro-Linguistic Programming, which can be another tool in your arsenal for combatting mediocrity, and helping your life be one of constant learning and improvement, by acting upon aggregated lessons of others.

Created by Richard Bandler and John Grinder in the 1970's, NLP takes studies from successful psychotherapists and their patients and maps the processes which resulted in positive and effective outcomes. By mapping what successful therapists did, the originators of NLP devised a repeatable and results-driven methodology which anyone could follow and get the similar results. Drawing on research in hypnosis, counselling, psychoanalysis, body language, language, and other techniques, NLP offers a combined approach to understanding why you do the things you do. By understanding this, you no longer have to feel overwhelmed by the decisions you make. It is a repeatable system which anyone can follow to get similar results.

What you say and how you say it can tell people a lot about your character. The amazing thing about NLP is that these patterns of language have been mapped and analysed so you can tell, with a reasonable degree of accuracy, what someone is thinking by what they say. Word-based language isn't the only way to gauge what someone is thinking; body language and eye movement can also tell you a lot. Being adept at NLP will allow you to understand others better, not to manipulate them, but to better build a rapport and trust. You will also be able to control how you come across to others, which will improve your confidence and ability to adapt in different social situations. For example, NLP improves your ability to say the right things at the right time, which is invaluable when trying to be the best you can be in situations from your workplace to your private life; there are few situations that can't be made to work in your favour through better use and understanding of language, and the subconscious patterns which people inadvertently use without realising.

I remember using an NLP technique (timeline) a few years ago, imagining myself in a beautiful flat in a white fitted kitchen, looking back over my shoulder to my nephew. I used this image as a boost to give me the self-belief that one day I would be free, and live somewhere I'm proud of. Within three years I was in the same flat as in my imagination (not quite as large, but with all the mod-cons I'd imagined); testament to the power of positive belief and thoughts.

Using forms of hypnosis to put your mind at rest, then using powerful mental image techniques to improve various aspects of your life, is a hallmark of NLP. I found NLP very useful to help me visualise what success would look like in the future. Because my brain has already 'virtually' experienced this success, I am more likely to achieve it because it is no longer an impossible, unimaginable dream.

NLP can turn a crap day into a good one by reframing your state and making yourself believe you're having a good day.

Why is relaxing important for mental self-development?

Being constantly on the go isn't what will make for a fulfilling life. Yes, the more things you do over your six LE the more likely you are to be having a great time, but without a break you will be in danger of becoming a headless chicken, forever running round without reflection or knowing where you're going. Relaxation is a chance for your brain to switch off from the usual routines and take in new sights, sounds, smells, feelings, thoughts, and so on. This break in the norm is like a reset button for your mind.

Being able to relax is also a sign that you are in control. I sometimes find it difficult to relax in any normal working week, because my mind is usually occupied with ideas, tasks to do, [positive] stresses, and challenges of modern day life. So relaxation for me is usually guaranteed during activities I've specifically planned to help me relax, including having massages, going to classes, meditating, and my favourites; weekend breaks and holidays abroad.

Holiday x time = relaxation

I can't think of a better way to take in many new experiences in a short amount of time than going on holiday. If you tried to fit in the number of activities people usually do on holiday in your everyday life, you would need to take the time off work anyway! So you have to get away, away from work and the usual demands placed upon you from bosses, colleagues, friends, family, etc. and give yourself a chance to unwind, while also being able to gain life points for the activities you participate in while holidaying.

Visiting countries you've never been to before is a sure-fire way to truly feel like you're on holiday. I recently went to Rio during the carnival period and it was like a different world; the people and atmosphere were totally unique. I enjoyed my time there greatly, and I genuinely managed to switch off from work (although I did check the odd email each day). Meanwhile, I was able to learn about the culture of the place, gaining a lesson on anthropology, history, art, architectures, food, and so on. I aim to visit a new country at least twice a year, as I know I'm guaranteed to experience new things.

My ultimate dream holiday is to go into space – and come back in one piece. I had the chance to buy Virgin Galactic's first space flight tickets many years ago but decided to invest elsewhere. They are now worth a hell of a lot more and in hindsight I should have bought them!

When you go on holiday, especially if you have travel companions, you will learn about yourself and others. For me, every time I go on holiday, my patience is tested to its limits. I've never been one to wait for things when I can see a quicker way. Queuing is the worst, slow-moving people are awful, feeling trapped is bad. All these things happen within the first a few hours of flying to any destination! So for me, I know I have to remain calm and prevent myself from jumping to anger. Travelling with a [romantic] partner is often the acid test to know if you are going to have an easy or difficult future together. Because if the holiday is filled with arguing, fights, mood swings, then it's a sign that you will struggle as a couple in future due to compatibility problems.

Physical self-development:
How can you physically be a better you?

Being a better you should be on everyone's thoughts. I'm sure you know, as I do, many people who never change and have remained pretty much the same person in the same circumstances. I think this is sad. Life is an opportunity to develop, and not doing this is missing out on the excitement a full life can offer. It's really quite simple to know how to be a better you. What things about you could you improve upon, or don't do well at all? The easy way is to look at your physical self and think how you would like to improve that. You think you could lose some fat and gain some muscle. That's easy: eat well and exercise using the FITT principles (Frequency Intensity Time Type). If you physically have things which are not quite right but can be fixed, look into getting them fixed. For example, I've been short-sighted for a number of years but didn't want to wear contacts or glasses. I eventually decided to have corrective eye surgery and the results were worth it.

If you have any injuries which are causing you discomfort, then get them looked into – just as you should seek help for any mental/emotional issues. Don't let physical niggles stop you from achieving a better you. I had a motorbike incident a number of years ago and left my damaged knee untreated. Over time, the injury developed into tendonitis, which was causing me much discomfort on a regular basis. I didn't think it could be fixed, so just lived through the pain (probably in denial that anything was wrong). Once I saw a physiotherapist, I was amazed, after many years of pain, how quickly the pain started to dissipate. It was a few months of boring, repetitive exercises on a daily basis, but it was well worth it to get rid of the pain relatively quickly.

For many, their physical appearance is what concerns them – they want what they view in the mirror to be acceptable to themselves and others. If you think there is something physical that you wish to change, which will positively develop you and grow your self-esteem, then go for it. I'm not condoning irrational and whimsical cosmetic surgery such as colouring eyeballs and bicep implants, but what I do believe is that you should feel and think good things about yourself. You will never be perfect, and the people who you think are physically perfect will disagree with you and list a number of things they would change. So your job is to find something that is consistently dropping your confidence and try to make it better. A good example is baldness. Unfortunately, there is no cure yet, and any topical medication will work very little and affect your wallet more than your scalp, but there are surgeries which can help you. Wayne Rooney (a British footballer) had his receding hairline fixed because it was denting his confidence. I would probably do the same.

What's all the fuss about a healthy body?

It's proven that the healthier your body, the more likely you are to live a longer and more productive life. You have seen documentaries that show geriatrics who have smoked and drank alcohol in vast amounts throughout their lives, yet are still going strong. Well, these are an exception, not the rule; they're lucky to have good genes. For the average person, high cholesterol, smoking, excessive drinking, drugs, red meat, and inactivity can lead to a shorter life span and lower quality of life due to the likelihood of obesity, cardiovascular disease, and cancer. It makes more sense to have a healthy body; even if you are not satisfied with how your body works or looks, as long as you are trying to improve it in some way, this will help your mind relax and focus on more important things. Your body shouldn't be a trap for the mind. The mind needs space to roam free and being comfortable with your body allows it to do that.

When you exercise, your mind and body are working together, and the feeling you get will give you further energy to continue. I go to the gym three to five times a week, and I get an awesome sense of achievement after each session. I feel especially pleased when I go the gym feeling tired and demotivated and come out feeling a million dollars. The scientific reasons behind this are numerous, but in simple terms, your body is releasing feel-good chemicals which help you perform better. This physical energy makes you perform better each time, while your brain releases adrenalin and endorphins. In sports, this feeling is enhanced due to the winning/losing nature of the game, but even in general gym training, each time you complete a workout, you are rewarded with a burst of chemicals, all free, natural, and harmless.

You will find that the fitter you become, the easier everyday tasks become too. You won't get tired walking up the stairs to work. You can go longer in the day without feeling tired, and so on.

When you are in tune with your body and understand its limitations, yet push it beyond what it's used to, you will gain an immeasurable amount of confidence. Your body is a vessel from which you can explore the world, but ultimately it is the brain which allows you to enjoy it. Therefore, enhance your body in ways which you know will give you satisfaction.

Exercise and sport

Sport can be both a pleasure and a self-improvement point, depending on the activity. There may be pleasure from winning or the participation, but in most cases it will be part of self-development because you are doing something which challenges your body and mind. How much it gives you in each depends on your focus, e.g. do you take leisurely swims with friends? Then you are leaning towards pleasure, and maybe some social points, too. Do you focus and rigorously aim for a hundred lengths at a time? Then it is mainly a physical self-development activity for you.

Regardless of your age, gender, or physical stature, taking up a sport and exercising is a vital component to leading a fulfilling life. The general sense of wellbeing after a gym session is unequalled. In a competitive sport, the sense you get when you win will spur you on to bigger things and boost your self-confidence.

Are there any sports you enjoy watching and would like to try? I'm sure there are. Some common ones like football are easy to find, as there are likely to be some well-organised clubs in your area devoted to football. Some more resource-specific sports, like sailing and golf, will need some research to find suitable locations and budgets. Some more esoteric and adrenalin-fuelled sports such as hand-gliding, rock climbing, skydiving, and so on will require you to come out of your comfort zone and embrace the controlled danger that is inherently present in these activities. The point is that whatever you have seen live, on the internet, or on TV, you can try too. I recommend trying at least one new sport/activity every six months, and to keep practising it until you become proficient.

If there are any sports or physical activities you do not know how to undertake, whatever your physical exercise goals, then take a course, or get a teacher. If golf is a sport you'd like to take up, then don't just buy the equipment and go out on the green. Get some expert coaching so you will get the best out of each session and improve each time you play. If you need that extra push to ensure your gym sessions are effective and efficient, then I recommend you get a Personal Trainer. Taking lessons from an experienced person will give you the insights into how to become self-sufficient over time, and eventually not require any help, unless you require a top-up in knowledge.

You don't have to be good at everything on your first attempt. I remember, when I was a child, being very frustrated that I couldn't perform certain skills with an expert touch straight away. For example, when learning to play the guitar, I would stand in front of the mirror and pretend I was playing in front of a large audience in an immense stadium. Then I would actually try to play and the sounds coming out were awful! Immediately, I was demotivated and didn't believe I would ever be good enough to play live. This lack of belief, combined with the usual teenage procrastination, meant that I never really learnt to play the guitar well, although I can still play a few chords.

Starting from the beginning is normal. Don't think that you should be automatically good at something on your first attempt. You may have to keep your pride and ego in check while you learn your new skills, but be patient and eventually you will be good enough to impress yourself and others. Fear of failing should not apply when learning new things. Unless you have tried and practiced for ages and you are still not good at something; then you can say, 'well I gave it my best shot and I don't think I'll get good at it'. Then move on to something else, if your thoughts are validated by an expert third party

Don't just give up without seeking advice.

Summary

- Self-development is the practice of learning and growing as a balanced person.
- Try to learn new things and improve yourself on a weekly basis.
- Challenge yourself both mentally and physically.
- Consider using therapy or other methods to help get your

mind and body in a stable place from which you can start developing.

- Experimenting is a key way to find new activities to add variety to your life.

Exercise

Write down a list of as many things as you can think of that you would like to do to get self-development points. Combine some simple things which you can start straight away and also some (realistic) dreams which would like to achieve one day.

> Visit 70lifepoints.com to receive guidance and support on Chapter 4.

The next chapter explores why your home can affect your chances of reaching 70%.

Element Two: Home

Feeling at home, at home

"Ooh, look at me! I'm making people happy! I'm the magical man from Happyland, in a gumdrop house on Lollipop Lane! Oh, by the way: I was being sarcastic."

Homer Simpson

Your home not only includes the physical place in which you live, but the area, town, and country too. Your home could be a room in lodgings, a mansion, a one bedroom flat, or a beach hut. The main thing is: what do you feel about your living circumstances?

- Are you comfortable?
- Are you safe?
- Are you proud of where you live?
- Are there things about your home that make you smile?
- Does it meet or exceed your expectations for what you can afford?
- Do you question why you are living where you're living and have regular rational desires to be elsewhere?

I used to be ashamed of where I lived, dreading coming home. I never wanted to invite people back, as I didn't want them to see where I lived and was embarrassed about it. This negatively affected my relationships and diminished my enthusiasm to make new friends.

I believe that having a stable home is the first step to a better life. It is the bedrock from which you are able to go out and explore the world.

If you feel ashamed of where you live, this will affect your mood and behaviour. I remember going on dates and not wanting the date to go well just in case they would want to see where I lived. So even before the dates, I was self-sabotaging the outcome just in case. My behaviour was therefore closed, dismissive, and essentially off-putting. I knew I wanted to have a girlfriend and make new friends, but my feeling of failure about where I lived was causing me to disturb the positive feelings I had towards someone with how I felt about my home.

So you see how a lack of satisfaction with the home element impacted my social circle element, my partner element, and so on. I felt in a state of limbo, not quite knowing where I was going or why I was where I was. It took many years for me to get out, and when I left, I realised what I had been missing; a base camp. Having this base will open your eyes to the world, instead of making you look inwards and downwards. Being stable means you can then think about the other aspects of your life. Without this base, you unlikely to reach 70%; although your base may be another one of the six Life Elements.

Your home should give you the pride and confidence that you are already successful, and can now improve upon and maintain that life. As mentioned, my home is the most significant element of my life, the foundation, which needed to be just right for me to base my life around. Now I come home and the view is spectacular, the interior is well laid out and designed to my liking, and the local environment has all the things I want. Essentially, I feel very satisfied with it. But I still want to upgrade one day! Why? I would like more space, higher ceilings, a music studio room, a home gym room, a walk-in shower, and other perks. So although I'm satisfied, it is good to plan for bigger and better things.

Make sure you ask yourself the questions bullet-pointed above and answer them as objectively as possible.

Enjoying where I live

It may seem like a simple question, but why should we enjoy where we live? The reasons are numerous, but I will focus on the ones which have made me who I am today.

Feeling comfortable about where I live has made me more open to new ideas and ways of doing things. I'm a different person to when my life was in shambles and I was living in a place I wasn't comfortable in or satisfied with. I still hold similar values and character traits, but I'm much more able to do things I've never done and meet people without being afraid or feeling second class. This is all because, at the back of my mind, I know I have a stable base which is not only comfortable but I have no qualms about. This is a very powerful platform from which to grow as a person.

When you are comfortable with where you live, you may find that your ability to socialise improves. If you are an introvert, you won't suddenly become an extrovert, but you will notice changes in your thought patterns, becoming more accepting of letting others into your life. Feeling pride and acceptance in where you live will make you want to share that with others, who may well be inspired by how well you've done. Do not underestimate the luxury of enjoying where you live. There are many millions of people around the world, not only in developing countries but in big metropolises, who are not living anywhere as nice as you can or are. Of course, there are people in much better places than you too, but I'm not suggesting you have the best home ever – as you long you are satisfied with where you live then you could live in a studio flat, boat, tent, mansion, or palace. It is your perception of that living space which is all-important. Without pride and self-esteem, your life will be much harder to find fulfilling and satisfying.

> **Key Point**
>
> Self-deprecation and self-pity is the enemy within and will serve only to destroy your dreams and aspirations. Believe you can make it and it will happen.

If you live somewhere that does not inspire you or make you feel comfortable, it is easy to fall into a trap of self-deprecation. Others won't see your situation in the same way as you, and you might be blowing any negatives out of proportion. And even if your living situation is as bad as you think it is, by beating yourself up about it, you are compounding the effect and will end up in a spiral of self-loathing and negative beliefs. These in turn become self-fulfilling prophecies, as your beliefs prevent your successes. Stop. Stop right now. You can and will be able to find somewhere better in future. How can I possibility know this? Because I have done it, and you have probably heard of other successful people who came from the gutter to achieve great things in their lives. The common theme is the belief that you do deserve to live somewhere great and have an amazing life.

Can I ever get the home I want?

You are reading this book because you know that your life could and should be better. You knew even before picking up this book that your life is not where it should be. You know that there is a way, that the successful people aren't telling you, to have a great life. But you're not sure if you are in the right place to start your journey.

Wherever you are, it does not mean you will be there forever. Things change, and by reading this book and following the strategy within, you are going to get somewhere you want to be and stay there. Change will be inevitable and for the better. It might seem impossible now, as you start this journey of discovery, and doubts will enter your mind, but believe me when I say that you just have to keep going, and you will eventually live somewhere better. According to Sonja Lyubominsky in her book *The How of Happiness*, you can control 40% of your life to become a happier person. I suggest that although this is a good starting point, you can control much more if you put your mind to it.

Imagine yourself in the place you want to be. Visualise this place and imagine actually being there. By imagining your area, your brain will believe it is possible (and it is possible) because you have 'been' there already. It might take months, years, or decades, but if you aren't working towards it today or stop doing so, you will never reach there. For a moment, imagine giving up, and being in a place you don't want to be in twenty years' time. Imagine how sad would that be. You should constantly be striving to improve yourself, and this extends to your living circumstances.

Without imagination, there is no way you will get to 70%. If you get bogged down in the details, and can't see the bigger picture, you will not reach 70%. If you can only imagine what you've done in the past and have no ability to imagine a great future, you will not reach 70%. This may seem harsh, but it is tough love – the reality is that if you can't imagine yourself in a better place, then you don't believe you can be there. You can also go too far with your imagination and be totally unrealistic. If your measure of true success is becoming a billionaire, then you will be disappointed. I would like to be a billionaire too, but it's not necessary in order for me to reach 70%. In fact, I reached 70% without even being close to billionaire status, and

I've achieved a deep sense of achievement that my life is worthwhile and worth fighting for.

Don't use humble beginnings as an excuse not to get what you want.

Where should I live?

There are many sub-elements to the 'home' element – What country you're in, what area, building type, building quality, neighbours, the way you decorate and fill your home – and all of these must be considered. So, let's start with the wider questions, then focus in.

What country?

One thing to consider is your compatibility with the government of the country. Politics will, to a degree, influence your life decisions, but you mustn't let politics control your life. I'm not politically-minded and do not see much difference between most UK parties, except the mess they leave behind. In the UK, we were recently left with Labour's policies on taxes, and with the Coalition (Conservatives and Liberal Democrats) we now have budget cuts, massive debts, and deficits. Neither party will give you all of what you want all of the time. You will have to go with the flow and exploit whichever advantages there are whilst avoiding the pitfalls of the ruling government. But if you are not able to pursue your interests due to restrictive politics, then it is time to move.

The society you live in has to be open to all. If you want to go to the theatre, you should not have to worry about whether you'll be let in, or whether you will encounter trouble on your way there. There are too many things you have to do without also worrying about society being against you. The society in which you live must be conducive to your freedom to be who you are, without the fear of attack or disrespect. Look around; what do you see? Are people moving around with their own free will? Is anyone around you smiling? Can you get up now and go for a walk without fear for your life? If so, you are freer than most people and already have a great starting point from which to build a better lifestyle. If you are not in a place where you think you can flourish, then you have to consider starting elsewhere. What's the point in hoping your country will change so you can start to grow? You have to grow and not bother about what your country is doing. If you are limited by where you live, then you must explore other places.

I used to dislike the UK, and especially London, for its bad weather, moody inhabitants, high living costs, and competitive culture. Now that my life is balanced, I've grown to appreciate all the opportunities that London has to offer.

Everybody loves the sunshine

A lack of sunshine can lead to S.A.D. (Seasonal Affective Disorder). It is a common condition that affects millions of people every year, usually coming during the winter months when days are shorter and colder. If you feel down throughout the winter months on a regular basis, then it's likely you suffer from S.A.D., as I used to. Ironically, even in a sunnier climate such as Spain, I still didn't feel great during the winter months. One method I started using which helped greatly was using a light that automatically came on thirty minutes before I was due to wake from my alarm. This meant that I wasn't waking up in pure darkness and subconsciously my mind was getting used to the lighter environment, waking me more peacefully.

I personally would prefer to be in a sunny climate all the time; I'm sure you've played the mental game of 'what would I do if I won the lottery?', and I would always think of living somewhere sunny or of sailing around islands in warm climates on my yacht.

So why do so many people live in cold, dark countries? Humans evolved to survive in the harshest climates around the world, from the heat of the desert to the cold of the Antarctic. Humans will survive anywhere and will thrive wherever they feel comfortable, in a temperate climate or cold conditions.

You have to feel great in sun or snow. The weather is changeable everywhere, but you don't have to be. You can remain stable throughout the year and take pleasure in all seasons. Taking multi-vitamin and mineral supplements is one way I make sure my body is getting what it needs throughout the whole year; I use the Usana brand of amazing products, which you can purchase as a Preferred Customer from my site here: www.70lifepoints.com/resources

Urban, suburban or countryside?

A big city offers many options to lead a balanced life and not having much money won't stop you from enjoying a plethora of activities and events, as many are low cost or free. However, if you want to explore and be an adventurer then you'll need some spending money.

You may be thinking that if you are not in the city then your options are limited. It is true that if you live in the suburbs, or further out, there will be fewer options available in the immediate area, but you will never be too far away from whatever activity you wish to take part in. And there are advantages for those further out: having a village atmosphere but being relatively close to a city means you are also closer to nature, which is something many city dwellers feel they lack (although London boasts a multitude of green areas, more than most other cities).

What happens if you live in the middle of nowhere? Is this book only for people in or close to a city? Certainly not. The strategy in this book does not preclude any areas, but certain areas may mean you need to make more of an effort to find nightlife, activities, social groups, etc. You have to face the facts of your living environment and be flexible enough with your time management to juggle any activity you wish to undertake. If there is an activity which you want to do but it is thirty miles away, this will obviously take you more time than someone who is two miles away from it. But the outcome is the same.

Basically, you must work out what *you* want and need from your local area, and then make the most of where you are, especially if you're comfortable there. Do not underestimate the importance of liking where you live. This is an important step to gaining true satisfaction from life.

I recommend looking at The Happy Planet Index which contains world maps highlighting global statistics on 'experienced well-being', with areas marked green being the most happy.

What if I can only afford a small rented room?

Don't despair. The Life Points strategy requires you to find the good in your life, separate individual aspects, and attribute points to each. Wherever you live, there are points to be had. Okay, you might not get to tick all the boxes, but you must find something good.

Before I created the Life Points system, I thought that I hated every aspect of where I used to live, bu there were some plus points, albeit not many.

If you are in a similar situation, then consider the same. What *is* good where you are? What can you do to improve your home, e.g. decorate, buy new furniture, etc.? Similarly, if your home is a let-down, consider what is good in the other elements of your life. If you assign your home, say, maximum 20% of your overall score, and you are only achieving 3%, then clearly you have to gain more points elsewhere. It will be unlikely you'll be able to reach 70%, because this would mean having to get almost perfect scores in other elements, but aim to get over 50% if you can. Then, when the time is right, you will move somewhere where you do feel at home, with 'home' rising to join the other, well-orchestrated elements of your life.

What if I can't move yet?

If your home isn't what you want and you currently have no way out, then you must ensure you are not letting it get you down. Use this time as an opportunity to visit new places. I remember when the thought of going home was the worst part of my day, so I would spend as much time outdoors as possible. Make an effort to see exhibitions, go to events, seminars, meet-ups, or whatever keeps you out of the home, but doing something positive and engaging. I would sometimes go to sit out in the park, and just people watch while I listened to music. I would play games in my mind by trying to guess the occupation, stories, height, weight, and muscle mass of the passers-by! Of course I'll never know, but I felt like I was engaging with the outside world. Being creative with your time will stand you in good stead when you are living somewhere you've always wanted, because then you'll not only have the choice to stay in but also have the confidence and willpower to go out.

Not being settled where you live should give you the chance to socialise more, too. Previously, I wrote that I found it difficult to socialise because of the mental constraints I had placed on myself in punishment for not living somewhere nice. But in hindsight, it is the people who I met during those dark years that I still know today and have been there for me through thick and thin. If I had shut myself off from the world, I would not have my small sphere of friends who I appreciate today. Spending time outside your living space isn't a form of denial, but in fact a show of character, ensuring you're not hampered by self-deprecating thoughts.

If you are finding your home is hindering your self-confidence for whatever reason, then the most effective solution I've found is to work harder. This solution isn't for everybody, but for me it worked. I knew I didn't like where I lived, so I decided to work more hours, not merely staying out longer, but putting me in a financial position to get out of that home, and improve my life. I wanted so badly to change my life that I knew I had to change the way I did things. My work became my life, which at times wasn't pleasant, but my methods were effective and I was determined not to lose. In fact, for a year, I worked almost every day; that's seven days a week with no holidays or weekends off. By the end of the year I was a burnt out husk and questioned what the point of life was – just being a machine with no energy for anything except work? The answer was that I had a mental breakdown; not a pleasant experience. I had failed to balance the work element with others, but the outcome paid dividends in the next two years, and a more well-measured version of this approach could help you too.

Summary

- How you feel about your home takes into account the local and national area.
- You should feel comfortable in your home.
- Points are allocated to various aspects of your home.
- If you're not satisfied in your home, improve it or move.

Exercise

Give the home element a maximum % of your life, then think of how many points you would give your current home circumstances.

Visit 70lifepoints.com for support and guidance on Chapter 5.

In the next chapter, you'll see why work is vital to your well-being.

Element Three: Work

Your waking hours can easily be dominated by work. How can you strike that all-important life/work balance and enjoy your job?

"The best way to not feel hopeless is to get up and do something. Don't wait for good things to happen to you. If you go out and make some good things happen, you will fill the world with hope, you will fill yourself with hope"

Barack Obama

Let's start with a definition: whatever you spend most of your mental and physical energy doing during your waking hours can be considered work in this context. If you are a student, then work is researching, attending lectures, completing assignments, part-time jobs, etc. If you are retired, then work might mean looking after grandchildren, tending the garden, writing a book. For the unemployed, it's looking for work by attending workshops, going for interviews, posting CVs, applying online. So work means a task-orientated activity that has a definite purpose and is rewarded in some way.

Without work, I would be lost and bored. It creates an output for my drive and creativity and rewards me according to how much effort I put in.

"If I have seen further it is by standing on the shoulders of giants" is an Isaac Newton quote, and how true it is. Mankind has created a world of wonder using our rational minds. Creativity, curiosity, and intelligence are key attributes that have brought men closer to creating a world free from disease, war, violence, and irrationality. This ideal may never be reached, but perhaps one day man will be at peace on Earth.

By working, mankind has developed into a race that is constantly developing and changing. Work not only gives mankind purpose but keeps the world moving forward. Capitalism has had bad press of late, but it is the drive of private property and personal enterprise that keeps the world moving. Even the socialist and communist countries such as China understand that work keeps the nation occupied and minimises civil unrest.

On a personal level, work should be something you enjoy doing and get a sense of satisfaction from, something that allows you to feel that you are using your abilities to overcome challenges and be suitably rewarded. I'm sure some of you reading this will be thinking 'what about the jobs that many people would hate to do?' such as bin men/women, sewage workers, or servants. Yet have you ever taken satisfaction from menial tasks done well? Cleaning and the like? Use your abilities to complete tasks as best as possible, and you'll get satisfaction from it, as well as being rewarded accordingly. Who is to say that cleaning toilets or brokering a multinational merger deal can't fulfil the same criteria? They are at different ends of the financial scale, but they can both be rewarding for the right people. This book will give you the insight to analyse work from a fresh perspective, which will make you realise your true character, ability, and potential.

Work typically takes up a third of the working day, not including travel and morning preparation, so of course it is an important part of life. But it shouldn't *define* your life; it could be anything from 10% to 25% of your Life Score, but no more, as this book instructs. Whatever you do, you should take pride in doing it and do your job well.

Where does work fit into the world?

In Ayn Rand's *Atlas Shrugged*, Ellis Wyatt said "What's wealth but the means of expanding one's life?" Whatever your views on capitalism and money, it is a socio-economic system that democratises the potential for producing/developing/researching in one's favourite fields. You may call me an idealist and say that not everyone can have their dream job. True – we can't all be astronauts and brain surgeons, but I'm saying that you can have a job that keeps you interested on a daily basis, gives you challenges that can be overcome, and rewards you accordingly. This concept is often lost, particularly on those who are lazy, or unemployed for long periods, and either forget the value of work or shun it completely.

If every human mind was constantly active and striving for exceptional successes, then eventually it would be possible for us as a species to develop into a peaceful society without war, disease, or famine. What I mean is: imagine a world with no unemployment and everyone working to the fullness of their ability, taking pride in what they do and being rewarded and celebrated. Mankind would progress at a faster rate than ever before. Technological advances would happen across biotech, aerospace, travel, etc., all improving beyond recognition because there would be more scientists, lab technicians, entrepreneurs, business people, and service industries to exploit research.

The world we live in today exists because mankind is curious and we challenge ourselves to build on our ancestors' achievements. Daniel Pink in his book *A Whole New Mind*, suggests that we've moved from an economy built on people's backs to an economy built more and more on people's right brains. That is to say that our ability to harness our creative ability to improve the economy is more prevalent now than ever before. We all want a better future, and fortunately there are very intelligent and productive people who are making this come true. They challenge themselves and we reap the benefits of that. As I write this book on my laptop, I remember just twenty years ago, when computers were still mainly desktop-based, and laptops were huge behemoths not quite suitable for the lap just yet.

Someone, somewhere, was given a challenge to create a device for work use that was also portable and powerful. This took the effort of the laptop case designers, the CPU designers, the power unit designers, and so forth. Moore's law has been continuing unabated since he coined the term forty years ago (Gordon Moore was a co-founder of Intel). When we challenge ourselves, great things can happen for not only us but for those around us and the world at large. Your job should push what you think you are capable of.

Mankind has achieved great things not by hoping that these things will happen but by using its minds to rationally explain the universe around it and assert some control over it. Without the human desire to learn, grow, and adapt, we would still be sitting in caves, drawing buffalo on the walls with mud and water. In evolutionary and psychological terms, the human race is perfectly designed to strive towards a future that is ever more advanced and suited to our wants and needs. Your work role in life should be part of this big picture and deliver the best you can offer to the world. Not just in the altruistic sense of giving for the giving's sake, but on your own terms, that bring you pride in knowing that your work makes positive changes in the world and makes you feel a sense of worth and self-esteem.

Imagine a world without the following endeavours of mankind's hard work and creativity:

- Computers
- Internet
- Telecommunications
- Medicine
- Transport

- Farming
- Education
- Architecture and construction

These are just a few examples: the list is nigh endless, and we can all benefit because some people have dedicated their time and energy to creating a better world for us all.

Where does work fit into my life?

'What's your job?' That is often one of the first questions that people ask when starting a conversation with a stranger. Why? Depending on the answer, this can lead to further questions and conversation. It can be a conversation killer too, yet even the most mundane job can produce some stories to tell. People ask this question because it says a lot about a person. But are they really asking, 'how much do you earn?' Perhaps they're more interested in how smart you are perceived to be depending on your job role? It's a combination of both, and more. When building rapport with a stranger, one subconsciously wants to position them in terms of respectability, social status, intelligence, and so on. This is to give the asker confidence and see if the other person is a match for them (whether it is a platonic or non-platonic encounter). But whatever the case, your work will be a big part of your identity.

What significance do you give your work? If you place work as high in your priorities as, say, 20% of your life, and you give your current work life 18% of that, i.e. you love it and see no reason to change it, then ask yourself this question: 'although I love my job, is it holding me back from achieving points in other areas of my life?' If you answer no, and you are able to reach 70% overall, then you're doing very well. If the answer is yes, then you need to see if there are any ways in which you can adapt your work schedule to accommodate your new variety in life, e.g. work one or two days a week from home, freeing up two to four hours of commute time to do new things. Or do something different during lunch break. Or go straight to an event from work.

If none of these solutions are feasible in your line of work and the other areas of your life are being neglected due to work, then you should consider changing your job. This is a serious suggestion that may shock you, but you are missing out on your life now. Life as it is now will not come back to you. This moment is lost forever in time.

If you are working towards something to reach 70%, then ask yourself, how long will that process take and how long are you willing to suffer for? You may be on good money and saving up for the home of your dreams, which you put as your top priority. Then that's okay, for a while.

> ### Key Point
>
> This book is for people who are willing to sacrifice mediocrity, compromise, and laziness, not for those willing to sacrifice a higher value life for a miserable career.

Or you think that with the money you are making you will be able to afford the home, the holidays, the dinners out, and so on. When will those happen? When do you want to start reaching for 70%? Your workplace is a big part of your life. But it is just a part. Your 'outside' or 'personal' life plays an even bigger role and will affect your work life. If you are not satisfied or fulfilled in your personal life, this will be reflected in your work life. Work will become more of a chore than an enjoyable experience, because you won't be happy in general. By developing in your personal life, you will be more likely to be willing and able to develop at work.

Is my job right for me?

It doesn't matter how many boxes your job ticks, as what is ideal is to have good thoughts about it and for it to make you feel good. You'll notice that this book doesn't delve into feelings much, as it aims to be as objective as possible. But we can't escape the natural human ways of attaching emotions to most things we do, and what you do as a job is no exception. Even if you have the most analytical and rational job in the world, you have a feeling about it. A feeling of excitement, or boredom, or emotions somewhere in between. It is a combination of the location, the wages, the people, the place, the role, the responsibility, the rewards, and so on which will make a cohesive whole in your mind about its esteemed (or otherwise) place in your life. Your job should suit you and your personality, otherwise you will always be in conflict with yourself and others because you won't feel satisfied or challenged. A good way to find out if you are suited to your job is to take personality and psychometric tests. One such test is called the 'Strengths Finder 2.0' which comes in a book and online test written by Tom Rath. Another method is by calculating your ROI (return on individual) as described in James Reed's book *Put your mindset to work*, which may help you determine whether you add value to your workplace.

If work isn't what you'd like it to be, then make it likeable. Create tasks that you know will excite you. Create mental games to keep you stimulated. Volunteer for extra duties which will add value to your working day by giving you the chance to learn something new, challenge yourself, and show initiative to your colleagues and managers. Work isn't always interesting or fun, so ensure that when it is getting you down you change the way you work, review what isn't working, and make a strategy for improvement. I remember working in a bar many years ago, and the work was incredibly hard physically and terribly repetitive. I knew it was only a stop-gap 'work therapy' period, but I still didn't want to endure the endless nights of either pouring drinks or moving crates. Therefore, I'd create mini games in my mind, such as counting how many drinks I could make in thirty minutes and trying to beat the record, or thinking about the jobs of the people who came there and making up stories about them. This made the time go by, and I remained productive and pretty cheerful because of it.

When you come to analysing your LE, it's possible that you will give work 20%, as I initially did. This is a high amount for any one part of your life to have, and you may even give it 25%, which would make it even more pertinent to give your job its due attention and efforts. Therefore, it makes sense that you look forward to going to work. I know when there is something not quite right at work, as I wake up thinking 'I don't want to go to work today'. On most days, I give myself interesting tasks mixed in with the mundane and frankly crappy tasks which blight my otherwise effective day, to make an overall good feeling at work.

Not everyone is in the great position to completely love their work and everything about it. In fact, I think that's true even of the jobs we think of as being perfect – for me, my top two jobs in the world would be Formula One driver or astronaut. I'm pretty sure that Mr Hamilton and Mr Alonso have had days when they want to crawl into a dark hole and pull their hair out, or at some points while in space, the astronaut is thinking 'what the hell am I doing in this cramped space with people I don't like!?'.

What if I'm unemployed?

In the UK, unemployment currently stands at around 6% (approximately two million people). In other European countries, it is a lot worse; for example, in Spain, at the time of writing, 1 in 4 people are unemployed. Is this endemic of the economic crisis, or something else?

Are you going for jobs where you have no demonstrable skills? This is a common mistake. You may believe you can do the job, and you're probably right, but the employer would rather take someone who has the right qualifications or experience in that job role. You have to analyse your skills gaps and fill that gap with learning. Remember that in major cities, for any one job, there are probably many people applying. This means that only the best matched are likely to be shortlisted, and from that list you may be fighting with internal candidates and those who are more experienced and qualified than you. It's a competitive marketplace, so you need to have the best ammunition you can to win the game. Show that you are proactive by engaging in side projects, and learning new things all the time. Some companies require CPD (continual professional development), but you should take it upon yourself to learn on a regular basis. Don't just read a book and shelve it, also known as 'shelf' development. Take action.

For the unemployed actively seeking work, don't give up. Give yourself some work points simply because it is 'work' looking for work. Ask any job seeker who is genuinely and proactivity looking for work and they will tell you that it can take eight hours per day doing this. Why shouldn't they get some work points if it gives them a sense of achievement? Even if that achievement is sending out the twenty application forms or finding the ten names of managers you can call the next day, it should be awarded points. This is not a long-term solution, however, and cannot continue giving points because the challenge is to find a suitable job soon, and if that goal is not met within a specific (and realistic) timeframe, the task has failed and should not be rewarded further.

How do I know what industry I should be in?

To get maximum points in your Life Score, your work life will have to be perfect. This is very difficult to achieve, but possible if you have picked the right industry to be in. Anyone who loves their job will tell you that their job pays them to do something that they would probably do as a hobby. This isn't realistic for many of us, but it should be your starting point. Think about what you do in your spare time and whether you would consider doing any of those things full-time.

Up until a few years ago, I found my interest in the world had diminished. All I did was work seven days a week, and felt like a robot, not really taking in the world around me or being interested in anything. In recent years, I've attained a better work/life balance, and I ensure I take regular 'timeouts'.

Too much of a good thing isn't always good though. For example, if your hobby is playing golf, becoming a professional golfer isn't an obvious or easy career choice. You have to be dedicated at a very early age to become a professional sports person, and that becomes pretty much all you do. For the majority of us of, hobbies remain just that. But this should not stop you from thinking about your hobbies and whether the job you have now, you would do in your spare time anyway, unpaid.

If hobbies are too esoteric or fanciful to become full-time careers, then think about other things that interest you greatly.

You may find that looking at what interests you will inspire you to find work that will keep you motivated every day. If your current job is not interesting for you, you will find that your days are drawn out and boring. You can't wait for the end of the day and daydream about being elsewhere, but this is the reality for the vast majority of the working population. It's crazy to think that we have many choices and we end up working somewhere we don't find interesting. Even the most exciting jobs can be repetitive and predictable though, but then it's your job to make things more interesting or find another job to keep you inspired. Your work drive is perhaps to be 'Motivated 3.0'; a term used by Daniel Pink in his book *Drive* that suggests you have a deep seated desire to live a life of autonomy, mastery and purpose.

If you aren't affected by whether the job could be your hobby or whether you find it interesting, but have the sole purpose of making a good living for yourself, then I suggest you go where the money is. There's nothing inherently wrong with working just for the financial reward, it's just better if you can have both financial and personal reward from the work itself. Being money-orientated is not a crime;

in fact, I suggest a healthy attitude towards money is to want more of it. Not just to accumulate, but to spend wisely and have that warm, comfortable feeling that making a lot of money can bring.

Going where the money is means thinking about industries which are known for high wages, such as banking, finance, law, and running a successful business of any type. You must also have an idea of your salary expectations and be realistic as to where you are in the ladder and how long it will take to climb up the leader board. Don't be afraid to apply for jobs, even if they seem over your head, if you think you can do them (but not *solely* this type of job, as mentioned above). You might just get the shot you deserve.

Am I trapped in my job?

It's not just joblessness that damages your Life Score. Say you run your own business and you're now a bit bored or in a period of stagnation or decline. The work doesn't interest you anymore, but it is still a good job, you feel in control, and you don't have bosses to appease. Stress levels are relatively low, compared to other management jobs you've had. You make good money compared to those around you, and you can save money. In this instance, if you value work as a maximum of 20% of your life, then you could give your job 10%. If you started to make more money, or someone wanted to buy the company for your asking price or more, then this increases points. Maximum points are probably not possible in this job because the job inherently doesn't interest you anymore. Even if you earned double from it, you feel that there is something missing. A spark that makes you want to get up early to go to work. In this case, you may also re-evaluate the importance of work in your life and reduce the % attributed to it.

If you are lazy or unambitious, and do not wish to work, then it is still possible to hit 70% (although much harder to reach), but you'll be missing out on the one Life Element that will provide the financial means to facilitate balancing your life with filling the other Life Elements. If you have the financial means to aim for 70% without having to work, then many people would say 'lucky you!' I wouldn't, however. I think even if you don't have to work, work provides you with challenges, mental or physical, that cannot be gotten elsewhere. For those dreading the thought of going in to work, or who have no life other than work, then this book will help you address the core issues behind your thoughts.

Luckily, depending on your qualifications, background, and career choices, your job is unlikely to be for life. It wasn't so long ago that you had a job and it was the only thing you did until you retired. A global economy, technology, and changing work attitudes have made many industries and workplaces more transient. Of course, if you are constantly moving every few months, this is not good, but every year or so can show ambition.

And on the more negative side: recessions hit the economy, forcing many people out of work and to re-evaluate their careers. Even whole industries ebb and flow so that few people can be certain of their job roles in years to come. For example, the publishing industry is undergoing massive upheaval due to the incessant progress of the internet and digital platforms, which every year are pushing down newspaper sales and the ad revenue that supports them.

Therefore, it is prudent to always have your eye on other job opportunities, not just in case, but also to hunt better positions that are out there.

However, you cannot think about what your dream job is and forget the reality. You have to think about what your work *is* and how far you can take it, realistically. You may be in a job that, even at its best, is not going to get you a top Life Score.

How do I improve?

Wherever you work, you should be thinking about the next level. If not, then how will you improve your pay, and increase your responsibilities and challenges? If you are not interested in moving up the career ladder in your current company, then there are other ways to progress, which I will go into soon – your personal development does not necessarily match the company's plan, but develop you must. Therefore, the workplace is for you to challenge yourself. Being promoted is a challenge you should aim for. I always felt arrogant for thinking that I was better than my bosses at doing their jobs and that I should've been in their positions. In some respects this was arrogant, but what it made me was an ideal employee who pushed himself to exceed expectations and deliver results. I was never afraid to apply for higher internal positions, even if I knew there were more experienced or favoured candidates. I had a belief in my abilities and made sure that my manager knew it. What is suggested though is to not be too big-headed, as this in itself can cause problems. I remember having a great job but thinking that I should have had my line manager's job, which caused a rift in my own mind which eventually caused me to, foolishly, leave.

So look at the situation objectively and ask yourself some questions such as:

- Do you work in a department?
- What is the next level above yours?

- Do you have the skills and confidence to fill your manager's shoes and do a better job?

Feel capable of climbing that ladder, yes, but work to make it the truth. If you are no better than your immediate manager, you are less likely to progress.

Could you be thinking about progressing if you are comfortable and happy with your job role? If you are, it could mean that you don't see the point in learning anything new or trying to improve your skills because what you are doing already fulfils your job desires, you enjoy it, and get paid accordingly. This is a good position to be in, but you could also be misleading yourself into believing everything is perfect. Without progress, it's likely that you may eventually stagnate and others around you may surpass your skills, knowledge, processes, experience – and thereby jeopardise your position. I'm not suggesting that everyone should constantly stress themselves trying to get their manager's jobs, and backstab colleagues at every turn (unless you work in Wall Street!). As Andrew Berstein, the author of *The Myth of Stress* points out, without stress we learn faster and we sustain our level of interest longer. But you should always be trying to improve and learn new things to make your work more enjoyable, productive, effective.

How can you improve? Attend management meetings. Take the initiative and arrange meetings with colleagues to make action points for improving. Go to workshops, take classes, attend seminars in your industry. Meet with your manager for regular appraisals to find out (objectively) how you can improve, what you're already doing well, and what progress you can make in the company.

Learn from the successful people in your workplace, and industry. If they are more successful than you, they are doing something better or different to you. Whenever training opportunities arise at work, take them. If no training happens at work, then ask your HR manager about training. Learn from your managers, colleagues, and your competitors. I'm not suggesting copying verbatim whatever your peers are doing. But taking the good things people do and incorporating them into your working life will pay dividends. NLP is a discipline that aims to map the successful traits of intelligent people and replicate them at will. In a general way, you can see what the people you revere are doing and do similar things. In business, I did not copy my competitors, but used similar marketing tricks to get myself started. Now they copy me – I take that as a compliment. If your managers are genuinely good at what they do (I wonder how many managers actually deserve to be there) then observe them astutely.

Developing at work is vital to you getting the most out of your work life. Work is the ideal place to learn more because you are in one place where you are required to be and therefore you can't procrastinate as easily as you can at home. If you don't train, you are less likely to develop and improve yourself. Developing at work is a matter of taking it seriously.

This is no different if you work for yourself, even if you are a sole trader with no workmates. If you work for yourself then ensure you are booking in for courses, seminars, workshops, and mentoring sessions, to learn more about yourself, your industry, and the skills necessary to succeed. You can analyse your performance and speak to people you work with to find out what they think of your service. Speak to friends who can offer their opinions, but remember to keep it objective and give them data to work with, not feelings, e.g. give them a summary of how your business is doing, what areas you think need development, and what you think you're doing well. Ask them to give some advice (even if they know nothing about business) because outside observers can often spot things that you won't notice.

Whether self-employed or not, your work should give you clear results, showing your progress. You must know your place within the organisation and how you contribute to the system. Career paths and progression are the rewards for good work and motivation to progress. A job without results must be hell. How do you know how you're getting on? You will learn from results, good or otherwise, and they will give you a sense of purpose and how to improve. Regularly having insight into the effectiveness of your working week will put you in a confident position to develop. Your job will spur you on to achieve better and better results, with hopefully better rewards. A results-orientated approach isn't everything, as the process can be just as satisfying for some. However, if you don't care about the outcome, then trying to have a balanced life will be harder than you think – because while you can enjoy the process either way, focusing purely on the process means you cannot analyse the results.

The glass ceiling

Quite simply, though you are not what you do, you are where you are for a reason. If you are in a dead-end job, you have put yourself in that position. There is no point blaming circumstances or other people for your work, whether you're employed or not. If you are long-term unemployed, then that is, often, your choice. If you are employed but feel you cannot get promoted or have no chance of improving your job, then you must get a job that you do like and have real promotion opportunities.

Your life is not going to wait for you. Time will pass quicker than you think, and before you know it, you'll have been in a job for twenty years, and won't have really grown as a person. To avoid this, you have to keep thinking one step ahead of where you are now. Every job you take – keep an eye on the market to see if you can upgrade. Being employed in the current economic crisis we face is a good place to be, but this doesn't mean you have to accept your lot, especially if your lot isn't inspiring you to work hard and enjoy it. You can sign up to certain jobsites such as Monster, Reed, and others to receive alerts when job offers come up.

What if my job doesn't allow me to progress?

If you feel stifled where you work and don't think that you have a chance to progress, don't despair. Keep trying until the point where you are sure you have little chance of getting promoted. Once you reach that point, this could be the best thing that has happened to you. You can start looking at opportunities for a second income. You don't have to change job, especially if you like it there, but you do have to *progress*, on your own terms.

A second income may be passive or residual income from a business, or you may freelance in your spare time. For many, including myself, this second income can eventually become your main income, which may give you the opportunity to go totally self-employed. The good thing about trying new ideas while in employment is that you minimise the risk of the new venture, because if it doesn't work, you still have your regular job. Another reason for having a second income is gaining a sense of control and freedom over your career.

If you are finding it difficult to get the top job you feel you deserve, then use your energies to save and invest in your future. As mentioned above, you may want to consider starting a business in your spare time, charging for your time as an expert in your field, or ask to spend more time working at home. But you should also think about investing in other businesses through stock or commodities, or investing in your education. You might want to learn a new skill, which will give your current career a boost, or indeed give you the skills to start a new career altogether. Nowadays, the technology for education is varied and designed very well. You might want to learn a new money-making skill, such as Forex (foreign exchange) or spread-betting. These, with patience and practice, could end up being just as financially rewarding as your job, if not more so. Do not be afraid to spend money when you have a clear idea on the return on investment (ROI). The old adage of 'you need to spend money to make money' rings true in many instances. This doesn't mean you have to spends lots; for example, you can start a business (in the UK) for less than £500. The costs include setting up a company name, domain, website and some set aside for initial marketing.

If you are not keen on starting a second income or investing, but feel that your job isn't as rewarding as you'd like, either financially, personally, or both, then you can take the option of working harder and smarter than you've done before. Eventually, your efforts will be noticed and even if you don't get the promotion you want, you will get recognition for your efforts, which will undoubtedly boost your confidence and in turn your attitude towards work. Not having the top job does not mean you can't feel great about the position you are in. You can still be the best worker in your role in the company. If you run your own business, you will want to think you are better than your competitors, and your clients will in turn see that confidence and good things will come. By working harder, you are proving to yourself that you are a worthwhile person, who is taking life seriously enough to put in the effort to achieve self-esteem and self-worth.

Every night before falling asleep, I get my best ideas. I used to keep a notepad by my bed so I could write them down before I forgot. Now I put them in my phone. My ideas tend to be solutions to problems I face or solutions to totally random problems which, for some reason, pop into my head.

Time is the most important thing we have, but how we use it is even more important. By spending your working day being as productive as possible, you are setting yourself up for a rewarding life and a mental clarity of purpose. This is the platform from which you will succeed.

Do I have what it takes to be an entrepreneur?

We all have ideas at some point in our lives – ideas are what have enabled mankind to thrive. Without ideas, you are dead. Your idea has probably been done before in another way, but your version of it is unique to you.

Any idea can be turned into reality with enough belief and energy. An idea doesn't have to be totally original or world-changing to make a positive difference to you and others.

You must believe in your ideas, especially if you want to make a living out of them. Your belief can't be rooted in fantasy but fact. You may have seen something similar work already, or you know there is a market for what you want to create or sell, but the underlying reason why a project is likely to work is your belief in it. However, the reality is that even belief won't get a good idea off the ground. I invented an exercise device called the 'HUB' which I thought would benefit many people. And it would have, but the market was not ready for it, or more importantly, investors didn't want to risk backing a product with no 'traction'. My mistake was spending many thousands of pounds on a product which I felt would sell, spending years in developing prototypes and patents and trademarks, when, in reality, all I needed was some pre-sale orders for the concept and investors would have jumped in more willingly. This is a lesson that, if you have an idea, you don't just need to believe it, you must get other people to believe it too, and use their money to show their faith in your idea. When you have that, others will follow. You won't always need investment, but you will need some validation of your idea, especially if it is a new concept that hasn't been done before. That's why it pays to build on the ideas of others but add a better function/service/quality/etc.

Above all, you must have the energy to see an idea through – and it's so easy to not follow through. I'm fortunate enough to have been able to push forward with many of my ideas, but so many are still on the drawing board to be pursued at a later date, or have failed miserably. I advise you to stick with one idea and put as much energy into that as possible. Better still, get someone to partner with you from the outset. You may already have a steady job and will find it difficult to spend time on your project, but it will be worth it. Use this project as a driving force to keep you motivated and mentally stimulated. I find that boredom is my worst enemy, and I suffer from it even with projects I initially fall in love with. So my secret is to have a few projects on the go so I don't spend too much time on one thing and lose interest. This might not suit your personality, but whatever you do, it's about giving it energy. When you talk about your idea to others, they will see this belief and energy and they will respect you for it. Where does this energy come from? For me it's the anticipation of financial reward and the pleasure gained from learning new skills, and new assets for wealth creation and self-development. I also get a thrill from beating my competitors.

Okay, so I could become self-employed. But can I risk it?

Becoming self-employed was not as big as risk as I thought it would be. I had made sure that my business was working before I gave up my full-time employment. Of course things could have gone wrong after that point, but with hard work and a bit of luck, I made it through the first year and beyond. It was a tough decision, but I knew that if I didn't try it properly I would never know if I was to succeed as a businessman.

You need a simple idea that you can implement without too many barriers, ideally based upon a business model you have seen work elsewhere, but obviously with your improvements. You don't have to be a follower, but if a lot of people are doing it and are being successful, then that's a good indication that it works. This relates to working for yourself or someone else. I always thought I had to be different to be successful, but this is not true. It's great to be unique, but guaranteed, nothing you do will be totally original. Happily, if it has been done successfully in the past, the concept has been proven, which should give you confidence in trying it yourself. 'Be A Better You' was one such company I founded because I knew I could offer the same or better service than the bigger companies did, at a lower price. I made sure the training venues I used were better than my competitors', and that the quality of training for better. This enabled me to keep the business growing, especially in the first year when gaining traction is vital to future success. Find out what people want and give it to them. Make your product look more attractive than others', even if it is very similar.

Using these methods, the risk of starting a business is greatly outweighed by the reward, if you ensure you are keeping control of your start-up costs and can start generating revenue as quickly as possible without outlaying too many funds. You will hear it time and time again, but your positive cash flow is vital.

As mentioned above, the risks to starting a business are numerous, but the main contributor to failing or succeeding is you. If you don't know how to get customers or sell once you have their interest, you will fail. There is a lot of support out there for you, such as your local government website, local advice centres, and business consultants. You should also take courses in basic business management and accounting so you understand about cash flow, marketing, sales, etc.

You may have a partner or other founders to share the workload. Your rewards will have to be split, but it is often better to have a smaller part of bigger profits, which is more likely to happen if you have a strong team with you. I learnt the hard way, and still find it difficult to find partners or work with a team, but I appreciate the skills that others can bring to a venture.

Once you have a business idea and you have roughly mapped out where you expect it to go and grow, you will already have reduced the risk involved in the situation. Many people start businesses without even planning what they are selling, who they are selling to, and how much revenue they want to generate. Crazy but true.

You don't have to put all your eggs in one basket. Give your business idea a try, but, if you have a regular income stream, don't give that up until your business is making enough money to support you, thereby helping you avoid unemployment. You can set up a website in a matter of minutes, and set aside a bit of money to advertise your services. You will find out pretty quickly if your product or service will sell. Set yourself some targets and a timeframe. If you have not reached the target in the timeframe, then you can assume that the business is unlikely to work, e.g. if you want to sell some fashion items you will be in competition with larger retailers, so you need to offer something different. You may set a target to sell four items in your month. If you achieve that you may try to sell six in the next month. At this stage, all you need to know is that your business idea works and is generating money. Another great example of generating income is network marketing – you may want to join my team as an associate at Usana Health Sciences http://tinyurl.com/70pointsusana

Other rewards for doing more work

Whatever you do for a living, there are rewards. The more rewards you receive, the better, and the more likely you are to remain motivated and focused on achieving better results.

You may have the boss from hell, but from my experience on both sides, employee and employer, the one thing to make sure of is being reliable. I made sure that if I said I'd do something, it would get done, on time, and I expected the same as a boss, when my biggest gripe with staff was unreliability. My patience was tested with staff who didn't see certain tasks as priorities and therefore either procrastinated, or took too long to complete them. This will make any boss agitated. Make sure you are known as the person to go to when work needs to be done well and on time. Your reliable nature will stand you in good stead when promotion opportunities arise. And, to return to rewards, you will also have a sense of pride knowing that tasks you are set and set yourself are highly likely to be accomplished and to a high standard – increasing your self-esteem and confidence. Your mind is your greatest asset, and if you are consistently giving it challenges and rewards you are going to lead a more balanced life in general.

If your job does not reward you as much as you'd like, then reward yourself. This may seem like a simple thing to do, but not enough people do it. For example; you reached your sales target for the month. Your boss just gives you a pat on the back. This is a chance for you to treat yourself for doing so well. Buy something or do something you've wanted in recent months but were putting off for some reason. Buy those golf clubs you've been coveting, book a holiday, get some new shoes. It doesn't really matter, as long as you link the good work with a feeling of achievement and freedom to buy or do what you want. Whenever I feel demotivated, I think of something I've done well recently and reward myself for it. There is always some good to be found, but only reward yourself if you really deserve it. Getting to work on time is not an achievement and shouldn't be rewarded. This is something you should do every day anyway.

Working hard will get you recognition from your peers, competitors (although you won't see this), colleagues, and managers. You should be aiming to get recognition, not solely because you seek admiration from others, but because this means you are, objectively, doing well. You may be a person who doesn't require the praise of others to feel you've done good work. I'm of a similar breed; I don't care too much what people think about me. I'm confident in my abilities and achievements, yet I find it easy to lose that sense of achievement when all I have for validation is myself. It often takes a third party opinion to put perspective on my work during times of success and failure, and it is always a nice feeling when someone tells me I'm doing well, because it is an objective measure of my accomplishments, not just because I can feel lauded. You should value the opinion of others whom you respect. It will give you great confidence to know that your work is recognised for what it is, and not what you think it is, which, regardless of how rational you are, will always be tinged by emotion and subjectivity. Your boss, manager, or staff should be the first people you are trying to impress, and by doing this you will invariably be pushing yourself to higher levels of achievement.

People will see you as a go-getter and action woman/man. You will be the first person people you know will think of when they think of someone successful. Your social sphere will have you as the epicentre, with others taking your lead and aiming for bigger and better things.

So, show the people around you what you can do.

> ### Key point
>
> By pushing yourself, you are more likely to be doing better than those around you and will therefore be recognised more for your efforts. And self-esteem aside, the more you are recognised for your work, the more opportunities come your way.

Pleasure - what should I do for time off?

It is vital that you take a total break from work every two to three months. This may sound like a hedonistic attitude, but it doesn't always have to be a trip to an exotic island. Taking a break just means a total switching off from work. If that means going abroad, then do it. If you are disciplined enough to stay at home and not answer work emails or calls, then that is fine; although it is recommended to take a holiday abroad as often as feasibly possible without draining your finances.

One thing you may find that you are forgetting when your life is as busy and fulfilling as it should be, is time spent doing personal tasks. This means catching up on those things that are on your to-do list but aren't a priority that has to be done immediately. However, the more things that pile up and you put on the backburner, the more they eventually clog your mind and slow you down. So every now and again, take some time off your busy schedule to do these tasks. For example, you may want to install a new bathroom and therefore need to research designs and reputable plumbers and fitters. You might have been putting off setting up a new bank account, or getting those new shoes you've been thinking about. Whatever it is, during one of your breaks, spend time completing these personal tasks. Try not to create more tasks during this time; aim to complete tasks already there.

Summary

- Hard work has made the world a better place.
- Work should be something you enjoy and give you a purpose
- Work, as with the other Life Elements, will overlap at times.
- Balance your work with a healthy life.
- Strive for success whatever you do.
- Take calculated risks to improve your position.

Exercise

Look at your job and whether you could be doing something better and more rewarding.

Visit 70lifepoints.com for support and guidance on Chapter 6.

In the next chapter, let's look at getting yourself a satisfying partner.

Element Four: Partner

Single and happy? Perhaps, but being with someone will make you happier still

"They will always be attracted to the person who reflects their deepest vision of themselves, the person whose surrender permits them to experience - or to fake - a sense of self-esteem"
Ayn Rand

Before we get started: I'm not a relationship expert, as you may have already gathered, but I'm trying to give you some simple tips to get you focused on the most important thing: *you*. If you are unhappy with the partner aspect of your life yet everything else is great, then fixing that weak link is important. There are too many variables for me to discuss all of them here, and there are much better books out there to help you. Just know that taking a few easy steps in the right direction is better than suffering the status quo.

The Life Points system and partners

It is up to you what percentage of your overall Life Score your partner constitutes. Different people will have different ideas as to what a partner contributes to one's life. Whatever you attribute to the partner element, perhaps when that person feels like an extension of you, and they provide enjoyment and fulfilment, then you have probably reached top marks for your partner element.

Does love make the world go round?

As the Rama-Kandra character in the film 'The Matrix Revolutions' said, "Love is a word. What matters is the connection the word implies". I'd agree with that, and add that the feeling of love is in fact a chemical response in the brain. These feelings don't even have to be based on things that exist in the real world, but could come solely from your imagination. Whatever it is you love, the brain is creating a strong chemical reaction to make you feel that way. Therefore, love is an arbitrary response to any given circumstance, and cannot be relied upon for 100% truth and logic. There is no doubt that feelings of love can be very powerful and give one a sense of great wellbeing and attachment to that which is loved, but beware that love can skew your perspective on a situation, and perhaps keep you from making sensible decisions.

Love may make you more altruistic towards the object of your affection, but love and selfishness are not, must not be,   mutually exclusive. Those who, say, cherish their cars will spend hours cleaning them, fixing them, making them better. If you love your partner, you are more likely to think about them and their wellbeing and do things for them. In my opinion, altruism can be dangerous because it's easy to lose sight of the fact that this life is about you. Your life is what comes first, and others are there for support, but should not be your main focus. If you spend more time on others than yourself, you will not achieve a fully satisfying life. Of course, others are vital to your life and you should pay attention to them, but you cannot forget that you are looking after yourself to become successful, not to be popular. Being selfish won't make you arrogant or egotistical. Being selfish means that you care about your life enough to give yourself all the things you deserve and to push yourself to be the best you can be. Relying on others for help, or helping others to make you feel good, is false altruism – there is always an ulterior motive to helping people. I'm not saying you should drop people at the first sign of them becoming needy or when you get bored of them, but be aware of why you're here. To make *your* life a success, not someone else's. You can help people to a certain point, then they need to do it themselves. If they don't have the desire, energy, or motivation and you have tried to help them, they will eventually drag you down. Being selfish means knowing want you want to achieve in life and focusing your attention on that. What you should be aiming for is a balanced and happy life, which is what I'm showing you in this book, and you will see that others have a vital part to play – just a part, not the whole.

You must combine your focus on yourself with the people in your life to get to 70%.

The stages of relationships

There are, as I'm sure you're aware, several stages to relationships. Let's look at them in chronological order:

- Attraction
- Dating
- Relationship
- Marriage and beyond (optional)

Attraction:

Who is attracted to me and vice versa?

Your looks are unique to you and there is not much you can do to change some parts of them, bar the drastic measure of plastic surgery. You have to be honest with yourself and realise that not everyone will be attracted to you. Even if you are what is generally considered to be good-looking and could easily grace the front cover of a fashion magazine, there will still be people who prefer a different look to yours. So the answer is simple. Be comfortable with your looks and don't let the world dictate what you think is attractive and how people are attracted to you. There is a TV show in the UK called 'The Undateables'. The people on there all have certain characteristics which many people find off-putting and unattractive, yet there were people who found qualities in them attractive. Don't be put off when you are rejected, because you have value; it's just that a certain person is not willing to give you a chance and is missing out on someone special.

Being comfortable with who you are doesn't mean you can't make an effort with your style. Your style will affect the type of person you attract. Wearing a hoodie, jeans, and trainers to a bar is unlikely to influence a professional business person to be interested in you. When I used to go to bars in my teenage years and early twenties, this was my usual dress code – casual street wear. It was comfortable for those long nights out and was flexible enough for me to dance in. I would see the pretty girl in a dress and make a move, but was shunned on numerous occasions. It might not have been the clothes amongst a number of other factors, but at least the clothes I could control and make a good first impression with. Essentially, be comfortable with who you are, but try to look your best when the chance to meet someone nice arises.

Above all, have you considered that your personality is not attractive to the partner you want to attract? It may seem bizarre and disturbing to think that who you are inside is actually causing people to find you unattractive, but this can be true. Ultimately, people will give you hints about the external persona you portray. This will be in the form of rejections, inclusions, comments, attitudes, and so on. Take these hints on board to see if they are hampering your chances to find a partner. I often found that I was very needy on first dates and was trying to get to 'third base' too early. I'm now more patient, and can decide whether a kiss on the first date is appropriate.

Is sex without love pointless?

Sex is a human urge which no-one can escape. You can train yourself to not think about it so much, but the urge remains. What you do with those urges depends on your attitude to sex.

Sex is a wonderful thing which evolution gave us to make us procreate, and feel great while doing it. The act of sex provides many physiological and psychological benefits, including the increase in feel good chemicals such as oxytocin, dopamine and adrenaline. Your brain (usually) rewards you for such activities, making you feel high. Your pain threshold drops, your mind wanders, stress is alleviated, and muscles tense up then relax fully. Sex is so good, in fact, that it can become an addiction for some people; and it doesn't always have to include other people. Masturbation is known to be addictive also. Sex should be a part of your life but not the main driving force. Telling that to a teenager will be hard, but many reading this book, who I suspect are past their teenage years, will understand that it's a natural urge, and yet to keep it under control.

If you have a busy life, and you are reading this to know how you can create more balance and value in your life, then I'm sure you will be used to stress. There are many ways to combat this, as I've mentioned previously, but one of the best ways is to have sex. In an ideal world, you will also have an emotional connection with your sexual partner, and therefore sex won't just be a physical manifestation of selfish desires, but also a way to express your feelings for each other, in a loving and intimate way. If not, then the act of sex itself can still be a very satisfying physical and mental relief.

Sex also gives you confidence. Being made to feel attractive is a confidence boost that is not to be underestimated. Of course, many of us have had sexual partners that were not, in the light of day, suitable partners, but who at the time, fulfilled a physical urge. But I'd hope you pick people you find attractive and vice versa. It isn't always the physical attraction that gives you confidence, but also the personality. For example, being with someone intelligent should boost your confidence because they find something in you interesting and worth their time. Confidence is a big part of this life game, and the more you have of it the more likely you are to get to 70% and stay there.

The disparity in attitudes towards sex between the genders is not as large as people make out. Men and women want similar things, just in different ways. But for both, sex gives confidence. People not having sex (not through choice) are typically less happy about their appearance and may have low self-esteem.

Keeping things interesting is key to a long-lasting sexual connection with your partner. There are many ways to do this, such as attending workshops and retreats, and reading books such as 'Sensational Foreplay' by Laura Ross.

Dating:

What should I be looking for in a partner?

You will have your own ideas about the qualities your partner should possess, and you will make your decisions based on these beliefs. For me, there are simple criteria which I need with a potential long-term partner. The first is attraction. The easy thing would be to write that they have to look stunning, and to some extent this is true. More accurately, I must be attracted to them – aesthetics are important to me, as they are to most of us, to some extent. This doesn't only extend to people, but almost anything; from cars to bookshelves. I appreciate good design whether it be man-made or evolutionary. So my ideal partner has to be attractive to *me*. Along with that, there has to be some sexual energy that keeps the spark alive, otherwise interest in each other will quickly wane.

Once the physical attraction is there, I believe that intelligence has to be a major part of the package. Intelligence isn't just the ability to think, but also to act intelligently and have intelligent conversations. I like to feel that I can talk about the most obtuse subjects and my partner will have a basic understanding of it or at least make an effort understand. I like to see a spark in the eye of someone I'm with. I like to know that they can think about what they're doing, as rationally as possible, can intelligently make decisions which are positive and effective, and act accordingly. Intelligent people are also more interesting. Try having a conversation with someone who watches hours upon hours of TV every day and all you'll get is why the latest winner of 'reality show x' is so great but not as good as the previous one. All rather common and banal.

The dating game

If you're searching for a partner, there are many options available to you, but which ones you use will be determined largely by your character, skills, time available and partner requirements.

The art of getting a date has changed dramatically in the past decade, especially with the massive rise of social media and internet dating sites. Some may say this takes the mystery out of dating and regresses skills needed to talk to strangers. There are still the usual ways of getting dates, such as friends of friends, or the typical bar/nightclub scenario, but things have changed and you no longer have to build up the courage to talk to the attractive person across the dance floor. I say bring on any way which lowers barriers to meeting your partner, even though those barriers are predominately manifested in your own mind and behaviour.

For example: speed-dating has come a long way. You can go speed-dating for very specific age groups and types of people, such as professionals aged thirty to forty. Or attend more fascinating variants such as silent dating (no talking allowed, using only body language and games), and pheromone dating (sniff the t-shirt of someone random).

Online dating has also progressed a long way. The great thing about online dating is that you can find out more about the person before even meeting; seeing photos and exchanging messages. Dating sites are now available for many markets; straight, gay, older adults, fetish, and many more. You have to decide what sites are likely to have the sort of partner you're looking for. Also, if you are rejected on an online dating site, it doesn't hurt as much as a face-to-face rejection. In this way, it is more impersonal, but the positive outcome can be just as if you'd met the person at random in the real world. As with real-world dates, you might be rejected, so you have to remain calm, patient, and keep trying.

Beware of sites that look like everyone is a supermodel and are over-friendly. Free of charge sites include Plenty Of Fish and Love 4 Free, but they are inevitably a minefield of fake profiles and dodgy characters. Still, you might find what you're looking for if you follow some simple rules:

1.   Never give out personally identifiable information such as address, credit card numbers, etc.

2.   Email suitable partners a few times to gauge whether they're real

3.   Get their number first and hide your phone number until you've ascertained they're real and you like the sound of them

4.   Have a phone 'interview' so you can check their conversation skills before going on a date

5.   Meet in public places

6.   Don't judge too soon

On that last point: the key with online dating is to have an open mind and not be too immediately picky. Yes, there is lots of choice, but many will not be suitable, so having a very narrow expectation of what you want will further limit your chance of success. Join a few different sites and send a few emails each week until you find someone you want to date.

Also, consider the friends of friends method; This is one of the easiest ways to meet people who are more likely to share personality traits that you are compatible with, as they are compatible with a friend *you* are compatible with. There is also the factor of familiarity and comfort. Humans are more relaxed and open to suggestion when they are made to feel comfortable and out of danger. Social media, such as Facebook, has played a major role in improving this method, because you can introduce yourself to your friends' friends and start relationships that way. If, however, you have a small sphere of friends, or very few friends and don't socialise very much, then you will have to look at other options.

Playing the dating game can be tiresome. Sifting through online profiles, trying to chat up or be chatted up in bars, or even speed-dating, is hard work. The easiest way I've found to find someone is being set up by friends. Being set up means the hard work of finding that person has been done already. Their personality has been validated by the fact they are in your social sphere (even indirectly) and others think you two will get on. Whenever you are single, don't be embarrassed to be set up, but bear in mind that your subsequent behaviour with that person can affect the dynamic of the group, and not necessarily in a good way. You may have family members who have single friends you could date, but again, do a bit of research first if you know nothing about them. Don't go on a date for dating's sake if you already know there is nothing there for you.

What if I don't feel up for dating?

Playing the dating game (and a game it is), isn't for everyone. Considering the LP system is based on reevaluating every few months, it can be okay for this cycle to stay single (if you've started a new job as a lawyer, or film director, now is not the time to begin a big relationship), but that in the long-term, you'll want a partner. You may want to have a more focused approach to meeting someone. In this case, assuming you actually want to find a partner, you could try a dating agency. An agency will filter through suitable partners more effectively, and take out the headache of finding dates – sifting through profiles and reading often boring text which can be off- putting, but doesn't really reflect what the person is about. Their fees vary, with some charging one-off payments, others a monthly membership fee. I wouldn't say you get what you pay for, because it really doesn't matter if you've paid or not, there is some luck involved in meeting someone who ticks many of your boxes. But it does take some of the work out of finding someone. They will also promote you to your potential match,

> I grew up in an unhospitable and scary family environment, so I learnt to spend a lot of time alone in my room in my own world of computer games, books, and music. Through a combination of nature and nurture, much of my adult life was spent as a solitary person who did not trust or feel the need for much company.

so you are given a boost before you meet, knowing that the other person already likes something about you, and is probably more serious than someone from a free or cheap site.

A great way to meet a potential partner without dating is at events and meetings you go to. You will, of course, have to make the first move, but at least you know there is something in common between you and the chance of rejection is probably lower. Some meet-ups are specific for singletons, so you are in the same boat as everyone else and shouldn't be embarrassed to make a move. If the outcome isn't what you wanted, don't feel offended and move on.

Even if your aim is simply to get married rather than 'date', you still have to do some dating before you can attest for the compatibility of the relationship. If even that is too long a process, you could try a marriage agency. Marriage agencies will set you up but there will still be a period of dating, which may be the perfect compromise – at least you know the intentions of the other person and therefore no time is wasted.

Key Point

If you are serious about reaching 70%, then you will need to make an effort to find a suitable partner and keep them.

Relationship:

Do I need a partner?

As I got older, the survival mechanism of locking myself away became less a useful strategy and more of a debilitating characteristic, as I was lonely for long periods of time. To have a balanced life, there must be other people involved. By no means should you completely rely on others, but you should have them in your life in key areas, such as having a partner you can trust and love. Do not underestimate the value of having that support, not just when times are rough and you need the moral, rational, and emotional support of a loved one, but when times are good too. Being single forever shouldn't be your life goal.

Being single is fine, and in fact many people make a conscious effort to remain so. Reading books such as *Going Solo*, by Eric Kinenberg, and *Party of One* by Anneli Rufus provides one with a compelling body of evidence to suggest it is, in many ways, preferable. However, without a partner, I believe your mind will not be able to focus as well on your self-development, because you will feel a gap in your life. Being single certainly has its advantages, but on balance, you will have more value and gain more LP if you have someone to share experiences with, both on a platonic and intimate level.

Your partner can also be your best friend, because you are likely to see them more often than the friends in your social sphere, and therefore will have more chances to interact and share experiences.

If you are a loner, career bachelor, or spinster (I dislike that old-fashioned word but its meaning is clear), you are missing out on the pleasures of having a partner. To get to 70%, you will need to amass LP from different places, and having a partner is a great and easy way to get them. For example, when you are with someone, you can go on holidays, visit new places, go to dinner, the gym, have sex; in fact all of the fun things you *could* do yourself, but having someone there will give you the onus to actually do them. Having a partner will give you points, not just in the partner element, but also pleasure, self-development, and social (when you go out to meet friends). So, of all the elements, partner is probably the most difficult to get right, but it can also be one of the most rewarding.

Take your time finding someone right, because if you don't think they have the potential to help you score lots of points, don't waste your time. For example, dating someone with no willingness to try new things, will put you in a quandary when you have lots of places you want to see, but your partner puts limitations on your experiences. This may seem too rational for some when it comes to something as emotional as your partner, but this book is based on reality, not the subjectivity of emotion.

Is my partner worth my time?

If you are single, then you are more likely to be open to a new relationship than if you're not single. This may seem obvious, but even when you are in a relationship, you might be with the wrong person, so it's logical to be open to a better, happier, more functional relationship than your current one. You should analyse how many points you and your partner are getting and whether you should be thinking about a new relationship. This may appear a selfish approach to relationship management, however, you should remember to focus on *you* and how other people fit into *your* world – that is the world you control.

I have proposed that you attribute a percentage of your LP to your partner, and how they fulfil your expectations. You must give a realistic amount of points, based not on the person you are with but what you rationally want and expect from a partner. You were given a choice of up to 25%. If you gave your partner 25%, this means that the partner element of your life is more important to you (whether you have one or not) than anything else, using this measurable, logical system. In this case, your partner has to provide a lot of value in your life to be fulfilling you and worthy of your love and time. Do you have the skills necessary to maintain and develop a significant partnership as the bedrock of your existence? This is an important question to answer, because, if you expect so much from your partner, you will need to able to deal with the points coming your way, and keep them coming.

If the points you are currently getting from your partner are less than what you consider to be a base level (e.g. less than half of the maximum partner life element percentage), and the relationship cannot reasonably be salvaged, then you have to consider looking for a new relationship. It is not as simple as deciding you need a new partner. Remember that it takes two to tango and you must be making an effort to engage with your partner in a variety of ways to get more points.

Thinking about it and acting on it are two different things. This equates to the 'grass is greener' conundrum; do you stick with what and who you have or do you risk losing those points for someone else who might well provide less points? This really depends on your character and circumstances. You may find it easy to meet and date new people, or you may struggle and won't want to risk losing what you have. Ask yourself this; is your partner stopping you from gaining other LP, thereby limiting your potential LS? If not, try to reaffirm to your partner that you need to maintain other activities and include them.

My partner doesn't make me feel good. What should I do?

You need to ascertain what it is exactly which is bothering you. Are you being too harsh on your partner by having:

- too many expectations: you expect you partner to do and say the things you want them to
- too much pride: you let your ego take over your decision-making
- too little patience: you don't wait for things to develop and improve

If you are sure you have done what you can to keep the relationship on track, and it hasn't worked, it's time to leave. Don't believe for one moment that if you leave this person you will never find someone better. You will only regret staying with the wrong person rather than leaving them – or leaving without reason. Remember that a break up may also be the best thing for them too. No one wants to be in a sham relationship.

If you feel your partner is worth persevering with and it's worth trying to resolve the relationship's issues, couple's counselling could be a good route. At the very least, it will open up communication, and you'll learn more about each other, and the reasons why there are any rifts. There is no shame in admitting you may have a problem with your partner. Remember that the aim of your partner is to improve your life (as represented by an increased Life Score), and if you used to get those points but are no longer doing so, then it's worth finding out why and trying to create a more stable LP-giving relationship. Counselling will show both of you that you take each other seriously and want to make things work. But you have to keep an open mind and be able to admit mistakes and make changes when necessary. Counselling also opens up your relationship to a third party, who should give you impartial perspective on the dynamics of your relationship and give you clues as to whether your partner is one worth fighting for.

You could also try writing a healing or love letter as suggested in John Gray's book *Men are From Mars, Women are from Venus.*

If you are in a new relationship and you already feel you need counselling, this is not a good sign, but it's still worth considering if it means getting you both on the right track for the future. A friend of mine asked advice about a boyfriend who, through his insecurity and lack of experience, kept dumping her, then a few days later begging for forgiveness and asking her to come back. I suggested they try couple's counselling even though they'd only been dating for five months.

Depending on the severity of the relationship issue you are having, you may need to report dubious behaviour to someone. In cases of systematic abuse, either mental, physical, or both, you should report it to the police or other protection agencies. In less abusive situations, ensure that someone in your social sphere or family are aware of trouble, as they should provide some support and guidance. If you have to report your partner to any authority, or are in fear of them and have to turn to friends and family for protection, then that is a sure sign to leave. If you stay in an abusive relationship, or even a relationship which drags you down mentally due to drama and emotional blackmail, this is again a good reason to find someone new. Don't be afraid to leave, even if the threats seem real. Staying is the worst thing you can do, because you are not giving yourself a chance to enjoy life, as stress-free as possible. A friend of mine had a girlfriend who did nothing but put him down. His confidence was shot to pieces and I warned him that if it continued, he would find it harder to leave and have enough self-esteem to find someone else. Eventually, it did end, but he wasted a lot of time and is now trying to recover his confidence.

Marriage and beyond (optional)

Why does anyone get married?

Most will say it shows commitment. Getting married is a symbol to your partner and everyone else that you are serious enough about the other person to promise it is forever. Of course, a ceremonial commitment means nothing without the mental and emotional commitment to back it up. But for all intents and purposes, marriage is what many people aspire to.

Love has not been mentioned much when I've referred to marriage, and I did this purposefully. As I've written previously, love is a chemical response to stimuli, which is fleeting and subjective. Basing a life decision on love is like saying I'm going to choose my next career based on the colour of the font used in the company website. Not to say that you shouldn't be with a partner who you love and improves your life, but *marriage* is a different thing. Las Vegas is famous for having a multitude of marriage parlour catering for overly excited lovebirds who take the plunge after a night of drinking and fun. Marriage is not to be decided in this way, and although love will have an influence on your thoughts, don't let it control you.

For all the pomp and circumstance that is involved in a typical wedding, you'd be surprised to learn that that is exactly what the bride and groom look forward to. The ceremony can be as lavish as a royal wedding or a simple registry office affair, but either way, for many the ceremony is what they've been looking forward to for many years. It is the fulcrum of their thoughts, and beyond the wedding, the realities of marriage often take a backseat. I don't understand this attraction, perhaps as I don't desire the attention or affirmation of others, which weddings inherently achieve.

In chapter 38 of Daniel Hahnemann's book *Thinking, Fast and Slow*, a study about the perceived life satisfaction of couples pre and post marriage, the author shows that after only two years, satisfaction had dropped to pre marriage levels.

Is having children necessary for couples anymore?

It is a fact that the human body has a biological clock which slows down certain internal mechanisms as we get older. One of those is the reproductive system. For men, testosterone declines after the age of about thirty, so the desire for sex, muscle mass, cardio-vascular function, and so on decreases over time.

With women, it's a similar story, but becomes far more complicated when it comes to children. The desire to give birth is innate, and increased by knowing that there is a finite timeframe in which to bear children. This biological clock has kept mankind going for millennia, and hopefully will for many millennia more. However, from a rational standpoint, not everyone should or must have children. Of course, if we all stopped that would be a disaster for mankind. But for many of us with the choice, consider this; is it really necessary to have kids? No it is not.

Having kids should be a choice made through a combination of rational thought and feelings for your partner. The amount of bad parents out there is shocking enough, but the onslaught of wayward kids is another problem for the future.

Inside all of us, there is a chemistry, a biological urge designed to make kids happen. You can't get away from it, you just have to know if you wish to succumb to the urges, or whether it really is right for you to have kids. Will kids add to your Life Score? They most certainly can if nurtured in the right way and if they have a stable family environment.

I never wanted kids as I was worried about being a bad father, needing to make enough money to give them a great start in life, and finding a women with whom I wanted to settle down with. As I've gotten older, I'm warming to the idea of having children, so time will tell if my family days are to come.

Did you know that some population experts predict that by 2100, the Earth will no longer be able to naturally sustain the amount of people trying to live on it? This is a scary thought: that in our lifetime we may see the effects of lack of resources even in the West and cities because of overcrowding and a burgeoning populace. Too many people are having too many children without thinking about the environment and the future. Does a family need five kids? What for? I'm sure you've read about families with ten kids, and of the ones I've read about, they're all on welfare benefits so they're also a drain on taxpayers too. The Chinese have had a one child policy for decades, since 1979, and they are still the most populous nation in the world. Just imagine if they had allowed their citizens to procreate as much as they wanted. They would be in big trouble right now.

Do yourself and everyone else a favour, and think about what your real reason for having children is, whether it is legitimate, and whether the children will be given the right loving and supportive environment they deserve.

Summary

- Focus on what you want from a partner, not what they want from you.
- Finding someone to date online is better than it used to and can help you find the right partner.
- Choose a partner with whom you will enjoy gaining many Life Points with.
- If your partner is not satisfying you, then communicate and solve, or move on.
- It's fine to choose to be single, but having a suitable partner will increase your Life Score.

Exercise

If you're single and in the mood to partner up, then start making some changes today; go to meet ups, join a dating agency, sign up to online dating sites, and ask friends if they know any suitable singles.

Visit 70lifepoints.com to share your thoughts on Chapter 7.

Pleasure-seekers will have a feast in the next chapter.

Element Five: Pleasure

How you can become a life junkie; addicted to life

"Excitement is the more practical synonym for happiness, and it is precisely what you should strive to chase. It is the cure-all."
Timothy Ferriss

My definition of pleasure as a Life Element is: activities that positively stimulate one or more of our senses, more than the norm of any average moment. Something that, if done too often, can become addictive and dominate one's thoughts and actions. It can be something that makes us smile (inside or outside), or feel a sense of wellbeing. From a physiological and neurological perspective, it is something that excites the pleasure centres of the brain.

I do not intend to list the different pleasures that any one person can possibly experience in their lifetime. Suffice to say that what brings you pleasure mustn't result in either a short or long-term negative impact for you or anyone else, or dominate your thoughts and behaviour at the expense of the other Life Elements, e.g. addiction to illegal drugs.

I cannot condone the use of drugs, but there is a reason why the 'industry' is so huge. It makes people feel better and/or different to their norm. For many people, drugs can take them away from reality and provide mental and physical states that give confidence, insight, and heightened emotional connections to their peers and surroundings. However, it is clear from countless research studies that illegal drugs (and more recently legal highs), can lead to addiction and mood swings, themselves leading to depression, crime, abuse, and involvement with other seedy aspects of the underworld, such as unprotected sex, trafficking, etc.

Therefore, what can be considered a pleasure? A repeatable and tangible activity that creates a positive experience without causing harm to others (and ideally not to yourself either). Even guilty pleasures are still pleasures.

Without such pleasure or entertainment, life would be a bland and seemingly pointless waste of our ability to think and enjoy.

Pleasure needn't be the obvious: a monk who denies all worldly possessions and does enough to meet his basic life needs gains his pleasure from meditation. A wealthy businesswoman who denies herself the trappings of wealth may simply gain pleasure from her achievements.

The last time I bought a new car, it took me a few weeks to find the one I wanted. A day or so before getting it I was so excited I couldn't sleep. I felt like a child at Christmas again.

However, in this context, we are referring to clear and 'bookable' moments in time. Watching a butterfly fly around then land on a leaf against a backdrop of a green lush meadow on a summer's evening could be a magical sight – but should it be classed as reliable, repeatable pleasure? Probably not. And even if it could be repeated, would you feel the same way each time? Would you still feel the sense of wonder if you saw the butterfly every day? Then what about sex? That gives people pleasure, but surely if you did it every day, the sense of exhilaration would wear off at some point. Perhaps the combination of sensual stimulations account for a heightened physiological and emotional experience that makes it slightly different each time.

Biologically, what is pleasure?

So we've gone through what pleasure is in terms of this book, but what causes it in the body?

There are many books that go into this topic in detail. One such book, by Candice B. Pert, entitled *Molecules of Emotion*, explains how endorphins are released into the bloodstream during pleasurable moments such as orgasm and why we feel 'runners' high'.

The brain is amazing. You can change your mood just by thinking about it. Your brain activity determines what you find pleasurable due to past experience, genetics, culture, and so on – hence one man's poison being another man's delight.

The brain activity for your pleasure profile will be unique to you. The unique paths down which your brain sends electrical impulses determines the activities you are more likely to seek out. For adrenalin junkies, nothing other than extreme danger will get their juices flowing. Rollercoasters are not enough. Base-jumping and waiting till the last moment to open the chute is the only buzz that works for them.

The electrical activity in the brain is one side of pleasure, but another is the chemical reactions that occur due to this electrical activity. Dopamine, adrenalin, endorphins: all feel-good chemicals which humans seek, and which make actions pleasurable or exciting. Going to the gym in itself isn't so interesting for me but the feeling I get from doing the exercises and subsequently finishing them gives me a buzz which I notably miss when I don't go. It can be as addictive as drugs, because the body craves feeling good over feeling tired and morose.

Brain chemistry can be manipulated using just the power of thought and belief, but many opt for the easier and more damaging option of drugs. There are so many upper and downers out there; I won't even bother listing them all. You'll have heard of the main culprits anyway, such as cocaine, MDMA, marijuana, and suchlike. Pleasure, for many drug users, can only come from taking drugs, and this is a shame because the body can do all of this naturally and for free. Well, free in a monetary sense, but you will need to make the effort to feel good.

Your psychological profile will be in some part based on the neurological and chemical makeup of your brain. Our psychology is how we make decisions on the activities we think we'll find pleasurable.

Your pleasures should be varied and not rely on one source. I still love computer games and do get pleasure from them, but I don't give myself continuous LP for playing games. I might give myself 1 point if I really enjoyed a particular level, but there is more to life than games.

Pleasures abound

Well, let's think about sensory stimulation. We have five main senses:

- Sight
- Hearing
- Touch
- Smell
- Taste
- (along with other, more specific ones)

Your aim is give each of those senses something enjoyable and new to experience. I find that going on holiday is a simple way to give my brain something new to process. Going to see a stage show or immersive film can have the same effect of transporting you to a different world – or even going to an outdoor restaurant where the food tastes better for being in the fresh air rather than being inside.

Another way to experience pleasure is sensory deprivation. This is most easily done in a flotation tank, where you lie down (sometimes in water, which isn't total sensory deprivation) in a dark, sound-proof cell. The only sounds you'll hear will be your heartbeat.

The only things you'll see are the spots of light we all see when we close our eyes. This does not suit all people, especially if you find it hard to relax and have a lot on your mind. But for many, this is pleasurable just because your mind is free of stimuli, and is therefore able to unwind and release stress. You can do this in your bedroom if it sufficiently dark and quiet enough, or you have ear plugs and a blindfold, but I recommend giving a sensory deprivation tank a try.

Sensory priority is all about focusing on giving each one of your senses a treat. The sense with higher priority dictates the activity and experience you will have. For example, if sight is the priority, think about things you can look at without other senses overcoming them. This could be done by going to a quiet art gallery, sitting, and looking at pieces which interest you for a few minutes. You will find that what you see will take you on a mental journey vastly different to that of listening to sounds. With touch, you could give or receive a massage. With sound, go to a concert. With taste, try eating in the dark (there is a restaurant in London provides that experience). The point is to make sure that one sense is given priority over the others, that you give it your full attention, and that you try to immerse yourself in the experience.

Pleasure seekers

Curiosity plays a big part in the evolution of a species. Being curious means that new experiences are sought, and with new experiences come new discoveries. Along the journey of discovery, humankind has encountered many ways to experience pleasure. Some are natural and occur on a daily basis, such as eating calorie-rich food, which increases neural activity in the brain associated with pleasure, and some are less natural: by experimenting with plants, and eventually chemistry and science, we have uncovered many ways to stimulate the senses using a variety of drugs.

> ### Key Point
>
> You can achieve pleasure in a cornucopia of ways, too many to mention and so many to explore.

Curiosity and the search for answers has driven the progress of the world to where it is today.

Evolution is the process of slow but constant change towards a better, more efficient version of that which went before, and finding pleasure is a big driving force.

In Susan Jeffers' book 'Feel the Fear and do it Anyway', she extols the virtue of saying yes to new experiences. Being curious is a good trait, and you can use this to explore more activities which may give you pleasure.

We are aware that some animals, such as dolphins and chimps, spend time playing, or exploring their environment with no obvious benefit to the survival of the species, although no species does so to the level which we do. In developed countries, we have enough free time after our basic needs are met to fulfil many desires. This is a luxury which should not be wasted or underestimated. You are probably reading this book in a warm, comfortable place. You are not likely to be starving, without shelter or warmth, and therefore you have the time and resources necessary to choose your desires and try to fulfil them.

Dangerous pleasures

It can be said with absolute certainty that even in the worst of times, it is pleasure that people crave. This could be the pleasure of eating, drinking, sex, an adrenalin rush, winning; but these can be dangerous in excess.

If you notice that the things you find pleasurable appear somewhat skewed from the norms around you, you may want to see a psychotherapist to find out if your pleasure profile is warped, and in need of 'normalising' before you attempt to give yourself pleasurable experiences on a regular basis. For example, if you find you are getting pleasure from seeing people in pain, then obviously you should not aim to fulfil your pleasure by hurting people or things.

It can be quite easy to fall into pleasure 'free fall' (especially if you have the inclination, funds, and time available) and start indulging in practices which are, to put it mildly, immoral. Take hunting, or, to give a more specific example, walrus hunting which amongst other questionable acts described in Michael J. Sandels' *What Money Can't Buy*, are what some people class as pleasure.

Risk and reward

Pleasure is about reward. Your mind and body are producing sensations outside the average scope of your daily experience. By that I mean that when you feel pleasure, it is a noticeable lift from the 'norm' of your life. This is not to say that your life is awful and feeling pleasure is the only way to lift you out of the mire, but that wherever you are in life, pleasure is a measurable lift or positive addition to your mood.

In *How Much is Enough?*, Robert and Edward Skidelsky wrote that pleasure in itself is not happiness, and I agree. Remember that all the activities you do in your six Life Elements will contribute to a bigger Life Score, which signifies a satisfying life.

The level of pleasure which you require to feel rewarded may require a certain amount of risk, e.g. as mentioned previously, you may be an adrenalin junkie who can only get the buzz of pleasure from highly risky activities such as unprotected sex, jumping out of planes, racing motorcycles, and so on. You need to decide if they are worth the risk, and these can and should be risk managed. This does not need to be a full audit, as this would require more time than it took to do the activity. But you should always think about the danger involved versus the pleasure gained.

I love racing karts and cars. This is a calculated risk I'd gladly take, as one of my childhood dreams was to be an F1 or rally driver. I'd also love to race motorcycles if I was good enough to get my knees down (will need to take a course first). So, many of my pleasures come with associated risk, as will yours, but don't just jump in the deep end without thinking about it first.

Consider: what is the risk/reward ratio, and is the pleasure reward worth the risk from the activity? If not, then you shouldn't do it. What's the point in undertaking high risk for low reward? Or even if the reward is great but the risk is even greater, then again, the risk/reward ratio is not ideal. There is no exact risk/reward formula that I wish to give to you because you will have a rough idea of how much pleasure you will get from the activity, and also the risk for you personally (a first-time rock-climber would be at a greater risk doing the same activity as an experienced rock-climber). It is up to you to gauge whether something is worth doing. I would say that activities that have risk should be done, but after research and with suitable risk management.

There is always someone who has already done what you want to do. Bar the few exceptions when an explorer, inventor, etc. have found something for the first time, it's probable that whatever you wish to do, it has been done. This is a great validation for seeking out that activity for pleasure. You know that if someone else can do it, then so can you. There are some things which require great skill and experience to get right, such as sailing solo around the world, and these may be temporarily out of your grasp. However, taking a sailing course is pretty straightforward. Then going to practice once a fortnight, then going to sail with a crew, and so on until you become proficient. So even if it seems impossible now, with a change of attitude and practice you can also do what others have done and get great pleasure from doing it. The benefit of others having done what you want to do is that you can learn from their mistakes and get the most out of the experience and avoid most of the pitfalls. Being adventurous nowadays is no longer the risk it once was, because there are many websites which have real reviews and guides from people who have done activities. There is nothing you can't do.

There's so much to choose from, what can I do?

A great way to keep up-to-date with the latest pleasure-giving activity ideas is to sign up to mailing lists of activities and deals websites. A popular site, which I have both mentioned and used many times, is Groupon and other similar discount and voucher websites. This is an American concept which is also doing well in the UK and throughout the world. The idea is simple; they have offers from companies which provide a whole range of products and services, from a bread-making course, to going on a cruise. Discount websites will have many different deals running every day and the prices can be reasonable, though it's worth checking out the company providing the deal to make sure it's exactly what you are looking for and that they are reputable. The great thing about these websites is that they send you an email every day with the latest deals, so you can check if there is anything which takes your fancy. This means you don't always have to think about what you want to do, as they will have an offer which you never thought of before, but you might enjoy. I sometimes stick to activities I know I'll like, such as anything to do with going fast, including rally driving, karting, supercar experience days, and so on, but also try new things I'd never thought of before.

Pleasure should be coming from various sources – don't rely on just one as it will become 'same old same old' regardless of how much fun it was to start with.

For example, instead of racing cars, you could try Segways, or quad racing, or learn how to race motorcycles, or take a trip to the Nurburgring. Use your imagination, but at all times think about yourself and what you are likely to enjoy. Pick a random activity which you wouldn't normally do, and I think you'll find it will add value to your life.

Mixing routine with randomness will make everything more pleasurable.

When it comes to gaining pleasure points, you will already have in your mind a list of things that you've always wanted to do, but were too afraid to try, or the opportunity was not there, or some other reason. It is great to have this inner list. This may even be your 'bucket list' of things to do before you die, but it's not necessary to be so extreme with your pleasure-seeking self. Not everyone wants to or will find swimming with dolphins on a weekly basis interesting. So whatever you already have in mind that you know or think will give you pleasure, that's great, but use your imagination to think of other things that you never considered before.

Create two columns and, in the first column, list all the things that you would find a pleasure to do, that would be deemed extravagant (or eccentric) to do every day. Then, in the other column, list the pleasures that take some effort to attain but are readily available. Example:

Special events	Regular
Hang-gliding experience	Sex
Holiday	Nightclub
Massage	Dining out
Music gig	Sauna
Sailing	Long bath
Track days	Cinema

Reliable pleasures

There is a science of happiness, but in my opinion, without control and repeatable processes, it is just hearsay. Pleasure, for the purposes of gaining your LP, must be something which you can control. For example, if you get pleasure from seeing the sunshine, then this is totally out of your control, unless you live in a perpetually sunny climate (not like us in the sun-challenged UK!), and so relying on sunshine to give you pleasure is foolish. Your control over the pleasures in your life dictates the amount and type of pleasures you require. Some things are easily done and can be done without much effort, such as listening to music, which is proven to stimulate areas of the brain which cause us to reminisce and feel good. Other pleasures require more time and planning, such as a spa break, or a trip to the cinema. Your pleasures should be repeatable, so you know that whenever you need points, there are dependable ways you can gain pleasure.

You will always have expectations about whether an experience will be pleasurable or not. Even if you've done it before, it won't necessary give you the same thrill as last time. However, as you know what to expect, you are more likely to get what you want from it. Or, on the other hand, if you are trying an experience for the first time, you should keep your expectations quite low so you won't be too disappointed if it doesn't give you the pleasure you thought it would. You will expect pleasure in different ways. Some will want an adrenalin rush from a bungee jump, others will want the calm serenity of a massage. Whatever your activity, expect to get pleasure but don't put pressure on yourself to feel that pleasure if it isn't there. I often thought a massage would give me pleasure, and many have, but some didn't because I wasn't in the right frame of mind to enjoy them and relax. I recently went rally-car driving and really thought I'd love it. Although I did get some pleasure it wasn't as much fun as I thought it would be, because the instructor kept telling me to slow down! I got more pleasure from the journey to and from the track.

Selfish altruism

You may get pleasure points from helping out at the homeless shelter, or giving to charity, but when you do something nice for someone else there is always some reward for you. The brain automatically gives you a 'pat on the back' to say well done. Even if it is a brief reward, you will feel good about giving, meaning true altruism can't exist. If you didn't give, you wouldn't feel good about yourself, so giving is actually a selfish act (as are all acts) to preserve your sense of self and wellbeing.

If you are altruistic in its most extreme form, being almost like a slave to others without any consideration of your own life or happiness, then this book cannot help you. This book is designed for people who comprehend that being selfish, doing things in their life which give them pleasure, is the only way to live – and these 'things' they do may, although not necessarily, include giving pleasure to others. By all means give, but by giving and not taking, you would be succumbing to socialistic ideologies which have been proven not to work.

In fact, you should be taking proportionality the same or more than you give in time and generosity, e.g. spending money on private school for your children may repay you in pride (pleasure), in better children as company (social), and when the kids grow up to be successful adults who give back a variety of LP. But you know that spending money on them now will pay off in future. Investments in your friends and family are more likely to give you direct rewards.

Dr Richard Dawkins, in *The God Delusion*, postulated that part of the human evolution story involved 'reciprocal altruism', our reward for helping others not necessarily related to us. If we were altruistic in nature, we would not have evolved. And societally, we would not have cared that our neighbour had a better plot of land, or a more efficient farming tool, or smarter children. Being selfish meant we wanted to be better than those around us and therefore strived to improve our lot. We should embrace this natural tendency, and wake up to the reality that being selfish has made us great.

I find it hard to get excited

If you find it hard to relax or enjoy yourself, you are probably not in a good place right now. You may feel jaded, cynical, and generally uninterested in life at the moment. This is fine as long as you admit that it is your attitude which is stopping you from enjoying life, and not that life is unenjoyable. Once you have admitted this, you can start the process of healing your mind. Your inner 'chimp' may be controlling you, as proposed by Dr Steve Peters in the *Chimp Paradox*. For whatever reason, your mind has decided to close itself off from feeling pleasure and left you in a constant state of malaise and melancholy. This means you will be neglecting one of the Life Elements. One method to overcome this is to undertake something relatively easy to do which doesn't involve other people, with which you can control how much pleasure you get and when. This could be setting an hour aside a week to lie on your bed with your eyes closed and listen to your favourite music, or trying some meditation, watching a cheerful movie, or simply having a bath. Nothing too complicated, just something to start getting you in the mood for accepting more pleasures.

If you are scared of trying new things, or of change, then you may also find it hard to get excited, because everything you're doing has been done many times before. Excitement and pleasure can come from the unexpected or the new, whereas fear of change may stifle novel attempts at pleasure.

Anhedonia is the diminished ability to experience pleasure, and as David Burns writes in *Feeling Good*, could be due an error in thinking by 'disqualifying the positive'.

Climb mountains

Many self-made millionaires perform extraordinary feats of endurance and adventure, which are usually a world away from their day jobs. This may be climbing perilous mountains, trekking through inhospitable landscapes such as Antarctica, or sailing or flying solo around the world. Why do they do these things? The first and most obvious answer is that the activities give them pleasure. But more to the point, the millionaires get the pleasure by achieving feats which are challenging. They are not afraid to push the boundaries of what they are capable of – hence their success. You should think no differently. Okay, they may have more time and resources to undertake such feats, but you can emulate the same thought processes and belief that you can achieve things you previously thought impossible. True, the richer you get, the more opportunities to enjoy yourself open up to you, but time doesn't necessarily come hand-in-hand with more money. If anything, the more money you are earning the more likely it is that your time is spent trying to make that money. When you have tried lots of different things to give you pleasure, you end up having to find other ways to reward yourself. Pushing your boundaries, regardless of where you are in life, is a surefire way to get pleasure. Furthermore, if you are following all the advice in this book in concert, your financial resources should increase with your free time.

Party forever

I remember when I used to go to nightclubs at least twice a month and thought that I could never get bored of going. As I've gotten older, I still enjoy going to clubs and bars, but not on a regular basis. But even if clubs and parties stop being your cup of tea, there is a club for every type of person. It may be that they are more intimate members' clubs, where soothing classical music plays in the background, or a salsa club where the aim is to dance the night away. But whatever your views on clubs, you should keep an open mind about the options available and keep them as part of your pleasure-seeking 'arsenal'.

I mentioned previously that I don't like to cook, but if I'm having friends round, I'll make an exception and try to cook something from scratch.

So if you can't club forever, what other options do you have to enjoy yourself? For a start, you can entertain at home. A dinner party can be just a few friends enjoying each other's company and having a nice meal – as the host, you can dictate the mood and tempo. However, also think about what your guests will enjoy. House parties aren't always the crazed drunken affairs one thinks about. Civilised and sophisticated may be the order of the day.

If it's a party you're after, get some friends round, put some music on, and dance to your favourite tunes without fear of being looked at as oldies – I used to see 'old' people at clubs, who were probably no older than 35 but looked ancient to me at the time!

Attending social gatherings is another alternative to clubbing. Gaining pleasure from social meets can be done by joining groups with similar interests to you. This has been covered previously in this book, so I suggest mixing it up by attending events with a theme which is fun, such as a quiz night, comedy show, theatre, etc.

Going to informal social meetings relieves some of the pressure of meeting new people. This is because you will have similar interests to other attendees, giving you something to talk about. There will be social groups for people of all ages, interests, cultures, etc., so you are sure to find something new every week to attend.

When attending social events, don't pressure yourself to enjoy them, but be open to new experiences and ways of thinking which you could add to your life. You will gain pleasure not only from the event itself, but also the people there. Remember that to gain pleasure points from a social meeting, there has to be something more than talking, which only grants social points. For example, it might be a social group which attends art galleries, or goes to comedy shows.

Hedonism

Is the pleasure itself the goal? No. If all you want is pleasure without taking the actions which earn it, then you are nothing more than a dreamer. Modern societies are based on the *actions* of people with dreams. Without those actions, we would still be living in caves. It is in man's inherent nature to explore and try new things to improve our existence. The pleasure centres of the brain have evolved to excite us when we undertake and achieve tasks that benefit us in some way. Desire is the precursor, the action is the means, the result is the purpose.

As John Stuart Mill said: "It is better to be a human being dissatisfied than a pig satisfied; better to be Socrates dissatisfied than a fool satisfied". Basically, there's more to experience than just the experience. An individual's perspective does not make the whole thing real. Another example: a rich family man who thinks that his family loves him and are happy. In reality, his wife has numerous affairs and disparages him behind his back. His children despise him but pretend to love him to get his money. Is his reality a true reflection of the overall situation? No. Each family member will have a different perspective and therefore a unique experience. If you aren't objective, you can leave yourself open to self-delusion.

Drugs are addictive

Drugs are a common way in which people try to escape their reality for a short while and feel special. Drugs are not 'evil' in themselves:

Washington State recently made the use of cannabis legal. This is a major step in addressing the problem of underground black markets, and the loss of millions in potential government revenue.

However, whatever you do, don't become addicted – you must remain in control. Recreational drug use, for many people, becomes more than recreational; an addiction. This is not what you want. If your life starts to revolve around the moments of pleasure gained from drug use, then you know you have overstepped your limits and should reign things back or stop altogether.

So what is all the fuss with drugs? I don't advocate one way or the other, I'm just telling you the ups and downs, but it's worth knowing why they are a route for millions of people to get pleasure out of life.

> ### Key point
>
> Being addicted to pleasure is a danger we all have to face, but something which can be controlled. You have been shown how to analyse the appropriate amounts of pleasure needed for your personality and lifestyle at this moment in time.

But regardless of how important you think pleasure is, it unlikely to make up the majority of your LP unless you are a true hedonist. The pleasure LE should be an important part of your life, but not the main priority.

If sex wasn't great you wouldn't be here

The human orgasm is slightly different for each person, and yet we all have the capability to experience it. The chemistry and physiological reactions which take place converge into moments of extreme pleasure which are hard to beat. Yet for some, it is not easily reached and often not as pleasurable as it could be.

Orgasm as an end result is pleasurable, but I think the journey is just as important and should be made with due care and attention. Masturbation is one way to get immediate gratification, but it is a poor substitute for the real thing. Your LP will not go up every time you masturbate, so don't think you'll get to 70% that way!

I suggest you find out what gives you more powerful and fulfilling orgasms, and do more of that.

Aside from what was described during the partner chapter, having a partner has one obvious benefit, in that you have a partner with whom to have sexual intercourse. A relationship without good sex, or with limited amounts of sex, is not ideal. If you and your partner have low libidos then this may not be a problem, but if one or both of you have normal libidos, then sex, good sex, should be happening on a regular basis. I remember having a girlfriend who wasn't very experienced in bed. The sex was awkward and uncomfortable for both of us. It got to a point where we were no longer having sex because we weren't enjoying it. The end result was that we broke up; sex is an integral part of relationships and of life, that you should not allow to suffer any more than, say, your health or work life.

To keep it fresh and enjoyable, experiment with sex as often as possible. Try different positions, locations, use toys, film it (for your personal pleasure, not for posting online) or whatever else you mutually agree on. One method you can try to spice things up is orgasmic meditation (OM). It is a method which is designed to take the woman on deep meditative and sensual journey that can lead to orgasm. The man (fully dressed) stimulates the clitoris of the woman for 15 minutes while she lies down (only the bottom half of body is exposed). The OM session also gives the man the chance to be at one with the woman and some control to bring about orgasm in a way not always possible with usual penetration. The woman enters a state of relaxation and meditation in which her thoughts wander, from which she will reach new heights of sexual pleasure.

Enjoying art – and varied tastes

We don't all go for exactly the same things – hence why we can each create such unique things. Let's take the pleasure gained from music as an example.

Music is great at setting the mood. If you want to relax, then you are more likely to put on slower, calmer, and softer music. If you want to dance, then you will put on some high energy tunes. Listening to music allows you to change your mood at will, almost immediately. I usually start listening to music after lunch time, as this is when my brain starts to slow down a bit after the intense work period from 9am. I find the music helps me focus on my tasks (especially the boring ones) and keeps me motivated throughout the rest of the day.

You can do the same – and it needn't be through music. We, as a species, are creative. We are the only species to create an environment around them which is not only functional but designed to have aesthetically pleasing properties. Humans have created art for millennia, starting from the oldest dated records of human creativity on cave paintings and objets d'art, such as jewellery. We gain pleasure from creating things. That pleasure is gleaned from the act of making physical that which was inside our minds. You too can gain pleasure from being creative. You may not think you are creative, but all creativity means is making something unique. This could be as simple as a bookend or paperweight using a sea shell you picked up from the beach. You could draw doodles on a notepad while sitting on the loo. Use a 3D printer to make your own mug!

Summary

- Positively stimulate all your senses on a regular basis.

- Pleasures should be repeatable and tangible.

- Your brain loves being rewarded, but don't become addicted.

- Try new things to find new pleasures.

Exercise

List all the things you enjoy doing and start adding those to your weekly schedule

> Visit 70lifepoints.com today for advice and support on Chapter 8.

In the next chapter, you'll find out about your social sphere and why it's important to get it right.

Element Six: Social Life

Your friends and family will provide you with support, advice, pleasure, inspiration, love, and value.

"Wishing to be friends is quick work, but friendship is a slow ripening fruit."

Aristotle

'Social sphere' is the important term here, as opposed to 'social circle', which suggests that everyone is on the same 'level' as you. That level could be intelligence, social status, physical attributes, sense of humour, wealth, or whatever you think is important, and some people in your social sphere will be above you in some regards, and some below you in others. Your social sphere is a 3D space in which I suggest trying to have as many people close to your centre and 'above' you as possible, rather than far away and 'below' you.

Being social is part of why our species has evolved so rapidly and successfully. The sharing of knowledge, collaborations on problems, and building on the past mistakes of others allows us to build better versions of that which came before.

Being social in this context could mean meeting just one person, or a hundred. As long as you are not alone and you spend time with someone who is not intimate with you (that comes under partner), then you are being social.

I can be rather an introvert at times, yet I can socialise with the best of them. I just find being around people all the time draining. I've had times when I've always had people around me, and whilst it was fine for a while, I started to crave my privacy.

I'm not a second-hander (Ayn Rand's term for someone who lives their lives through the validations and viewpoints of others), but I'm aware that, without social interactions, life can be boring, and I'd be limited in my potential to meet people, make friends, get new ideas, and have fun.

The parts of a social life

Once again, let's take this step-by-step, with loose categories for looking at the parts of a social life.

- Your social skills
- Your social sphere
- Social events
- Why mix with others?
- Social family

Your social skills:

Why am I sociable/not sociable?

How you were brought up will have played a significant part in your social development. A 'normal' household, with two reasonably balanced parents, in a 'normal' area with low levels of crime and friendly neighbours may have given you chance to develop a normal ability to socialise. Normal will mean different things to different people, but what I mean is that growing up with a balanced social network and supportive and sociable parents means you are more likely to be sociable, even if genetically you might be predisposed to being introverted and unsociable.

I remember being very sociable as a child, up to about the age of ten, after which time the negative circumstances of the household started to affect my behaviour. Prior to that I was gregarious, outgoing, a bit of a buffoon, but always popular and able to talk to everyone. I think this was because I had no experience of fear, and therefore no fear of rejection or need to protect my ego.

It's quite possible that you have the most sociable parents, siblings, friends, and a safe upbringing, and yet you remain unsociable or even anti-social. This could be a genetic characteristic that has influenced your demeanour, overriding cultural and nurturing stimulation. Is there anything you can do about it? To a degree – start by understanding it and make an effort to engage with others as often as you can. I've met real introverts before, and it's very clear that their need to be in their own space becomes more important than being around people. But as mentioned before, if you are not very sociable you are missing out on valuable points to help you get to 70%. It will be harder for you to reach it alone (although not impossible) so perhaps you could try some of the suggestions made above to start getting you out of your shell and mingling, one step at a time.

Socialite

A few tips to help you on your way to being a more sociable person. The first is to be complimentary. It is often overlooked, especially by men, but it is a powerful tool to make people feel good about themselves. I don't usually compliment, as I find the process to be a bit embarrassing. I also don't take compliments very well, as I don't usually trust the person's motives (even though I probably believe the compliment!). This is just my suspicious and cynical viewpoint, especially when meeting new people. But I do remember compliments very well. In fact, I remember going to a seminar and, after the presenter had finished, I went to talk to him. The first thing he did was shake my hand and compliment me on my firm handshake and my watch. I was slightly taken aback, as I wasn't expecting that, particularly from a guy, and I knew it was a tactic to make me feel comfortable straight away, but it worked and I still remember it.

Being sociable means engaging with others, ideally not superficially, but finding out a bit about what makes them tick and their everyday lives. You will see, in the next chapters, what constitutes a social point, but suffice to say here that if you are just nodding 'hi' and having very shallow chitchat, you will not get any points. You must find out some personal things: hopes, aspirations, and get to know the other person as deeply as you can without appearing intrusive or entering their private space.

Engaging also requires energy and willingness. I've been to many events where I wasn't really in the mood to mingle but was still fascinated and engaged by the main event. If you are not naturally empathetic, it's quite simple to fake it. Keep asking questions about the other person, but remember the answers and respond accordingly.

> ### Key Point
>
> You don't necessarily have to treat each person you meet as a challenge, but try to engage with as many different people as possible, as this broadens your skills and capacity to learn.

What things will get my social skills working?

If you fancy a challenge, you could attend a debate on a subject which you feel passionate about. These sorts of debates, where the subject matter is both fascinating and complex, can help you practice your social and conversational skills. Always talking to the same people about the same things does not give your brain a chance to grow and develop new ways of thinking and doing things. Therefore, debates are great to get the mental juices flowing. Even if you are not confident enough to offer your opinions to the group at large, you can always speak to individuals before or afterwards, to voice your opinions and hear their perspectives. When you build up confidence from these debates, you can start to voice your thoughts to the group, which will also help both with speaking to other groups and with public speaking in future.

Entering public competitions is another great way to meet new people and improve your conversational skills. The competitions could be sports-related, such as 'park runs', where groups put up their best times for running 5km around a park. The competitive edge may give you that boost you need to come out of your shell and take on the world. Look for competitions where the entrants either meet during the selection process or meet up once shortlisted. I find that any time I have to beat the people around me, I get chattier. Most likely I'm trying to gauge who my true competition is and also employ some scare tactics to unsettle my opponents, but still, it's a good way to get yourself in social mode through competition. At the other end of the spectrum, eating challenges are a favourite for many. Not especially healthy, but man vs food clones are in many places, and you could meet friends that way.

Try to organise events with friends. It could be as simple as a picnic in the park, or a holiday, or a day out somewhere. It doesn't really matter what it is, as long as you get a chance to work and collaborate as a social team.

Do extroverts have all the fun?

You may have already gathered that, although I'm far from shy or lacking confidence, I err on the side of caution when it comes to meeting new people and can seem more introvert than extrovert at times. This doesn't seem the case for people who know me or when

I've had a few drinks, but in general I would say I'm about halfway between introvert and extrovert. True extroverts, who are pretty much the same with whoever they meet, are a mystery to me. I don't understand how they can talk to strangers so easily without any fear of rejection or time-wasting.

Extroverts will tend to have larger social networks and the ability to mingle is second nature to them. I'm not so sure this is a trait which can be learnt, but more a genetic and cultural force. I've always wondered if extroverts, especially those who have large social spheres, have substance. I couldn't imagine how someone who talks to so many people on a regular basis can know enough information about each person to make it worthwhile.

Being uninhibited when it comes to being social is a great trait to have, especially if you're able to combine that with meaningful and long-lasting conversation which leads to fulfilling friendships and more.

Your social sphere:

Groupthink

We all want to feel comfortable with who we socialise with. This instinct is normal and in everyone's interest. Why? Because feeling comfortable implies that you feel safe. Feeling safe from what, it's hard to say, but it could be from harm, social exclusion, social embarrassment, and so on. The fear you have of being in a group of people who are very different to you stems from your mind's natural tendency to be wary of things you don't know. This is a common human trait, and there is not much you can do to suppress it except to embrace new social connections, and try to accept their idiosyncrasies and sensibilities. Is the fear justified? I believe so, but can also be an error in your way of thinking that is limiting your social experiences.

Who you feel more comfortable with will in turn dictate the types of people you mix with. Is the average person on the street likely to socialise with royalty? No. Royalty will have their own social sphere in which they feel most comfortable. They would not mingle with the average Joe in the street, because that is not their area – where they live. Would you feel comfortable chilling with the Queen? I wouldn't, as it's unlikely we have much in common, and besides, I don't believe the world needs any monarchies so that would be quite an awkward conversation to have! When you are out, you are going to gravitate to people you think are like you, rather than those who are different. This isn't wrong; it's human instinct to flock in tribes.

However, by allowing your fear of new types of people to dictate your social sphere, you can end up with a 'social line' of friends who do similar things to you, say similar things, and wear the same things; creating a superficial world where you have no experiences of other personalities. The severity of this effect is affected by your personality, in the sense that if you are naturally sociable and open, you are more likely to have a diverse social group, whereas if you are more insular, afraid of new things and people, you will likely gravitate to a more homogenised social sphere.

Peer pressure is very powerful, as what you think others are thinking about you – which *is* something we all consider to varying degrees – can significantly influence your choice of friends. Some are more prone to be persuaded and influenced by outside sources. Pressure can be obvious, but is usually subtle, with quiet comments and negative opinions about the new friend, even if the commenter has never met the new friend. These 'commenter' types of people will only have friends who they think their other friends will like. I think this limits your social sphere to a shallow level, whereby your choices are based on what you think others will think, and not your own independent judgement. Even pressure to be different and have friends from all walks of life is negative, as again you are being influenced rather than doing what you actually need in your life.

Limited social sphere

You should not feel bad about who you don't know. There is a reason you have the social sphere you have and there is no reason to change that unless you think you have made a mistake in rejecting someone who could have been good for you, or allowing someone in who is bad for you.

Where you were brought up, where you live, and where you work will influence your social sphere, and there is no need to apologise for that. However, if you think you are limited and missing out on the valuable insights and support different cultures can offer, then perhaps you need to expand your social sphere.

As you grow up, you are put in groups. This will be in school, family gatherings, birthday parties, holidays, and so on. Each experience you have with other people shapes your social choices in the future, because you'll feel safer choosing types of people you have had experience with before as friends. Therefore, your culture will dictate, at least through to your early adulthood, your social choices. As you become a more independent adult, you will have more choices as to whom you socialise with. But as your culture will have, to a certain extent, 'indoctrinated' you, your apparently 'free choices' are not actually so. You will have unconsciously already made choices about who you feel comfortable with, and your behaviour will follow these beliefs.

Snap judgments are one of my many failings when it comes to social interactions. My lack of patience (which has improved in recent years, but is still too short for my liking) causes me to get bored of people very quickly if I don't see an opportunity in one way or another. By 'opportunity', I mean that the other person may have ideas I like, or a job I find fascinating, or a sense of humour I like, and so on.

There is no doubt that the amount of money you make can also influence your choice of friends. As you move up the career and salary ladder, you will find that your tastes change, your expectations increase, and your tolerance for mediocrity decreases. This is because you start to notice things you do differently to people with lower incomes. This could be something as simple as buying expensive underwear, or having a flashy car and going on expensive holidays. Therefore, you may prefer people who are on a similar financial level, or above, to keep you motivated and interested. We all want to think that we are surrounding ourselves with people with similar sensibilities and achievements to our own, as this gives us perspective on our own lives.

However, I think you need to be aware of this conditioning and analyse whether these old beliefs are indeed limiting or giving you the value you need to achieve 70%. No-one else will be able to tell you who you should have in your social sphere, and it's also not so easy just to say who you are going to have as friends, as this is usually determined organically and unpredictably.

How do I know if someone is a good fit for me?

Patience is key when it comes to meeting new people. You have to wait for them to divulge information before you make a judgement as to whether they will add value to your life. Being impatient means that you are not giving people or yourself time to get to know each other and find out what makes each other tick. Making new friends and developing current friendships takes an unhurried approach, even though you might think that you can tell straight away if you like someone or not. Maybe you can, but you can also make snap judgements which don't give you any opportunity to learn about the person.

Take your time with new people and get their contact details, to see if a friendship can develop.

Do I know who my friends really are?

I think friends are there for various reasons, but the most important is support. Life is a challenge and you need the right people to share your problems with. Trying to 'do' life alone is much like trying to climb a mountain by yourself: frightening, lonely, and the risk of failing is higher. You don't need to have loads of friends to have the right support network you need to succeed in life, just the right type of people, whom you know you can count on for support and advice in times of need and stress. A good friend will know when you are in a good mood and also when you're feeling down, and be able to act accordingly.

Friends have to communicate. There is no point having a friend if you speak and contact each other once a year or less. There may be 'friends' from your childhood who have moved away or diverged from your lifestyle to new places. These are no longer friends, no longer members of your social sphere, but past acquaintances. There is not much point in trying to rekindle these types of friendships unless you are able to start communicating on a regular basis. My friends often tell me I don't contact them enough, and they are right. But what I tell them is that the reason that they are my friends is because they are more sociable than me and are able to contact me more regularly than I contact them. Which means that we still engage frequently, but they usually instigate the communication. To a certain extent, they are fine with this, because they are comfortable with contacting their friends, while I don't do it as easily, so our personalities complement each other well. They know I'm thinking about them and will always have time for them, but they also know I'm busy and don't tend to contact people on a regular basis (although I am improving in this area).

Keeping up with friends 'virtually' is still a useful way to remain in contact with people who may not be in your local area. Facebook is a common portal through which you can remain friends with people you've met on holiday or in places where you used to live, etc., keeping the relationship or useful connection alive until you can meet up next.

Whatever type of person you are, there needs to be reasonable regular interaction in your social sphere, to keep up-to-date with life developments, show interest in your friends' lives, and offer the support and advice they also like from you.

Socialising at work

Your workplace is a great source of friends. You are with your co-workers for eight hours a day, and you are on similar career paths, so this is a common theme from which you can develop friendships.

The one problem I've found with trying to socialise at work is tiredness. Whenever I was invited to drinks after work (when I used to work for other companies), I usually declined because I was tired and just wanted to go home and eat. In hindsight, I regret choosing to miss out on these opportunities for socialising. They could've made my workplace a more comfortable environment, as they can for you, giving you a wider support network, but also potential friends for life.

So, make an effort to go out with workmates. If you know they are likely to ask you to go out on a Friday night, make sure you've had a good sleep the night before and free up some time.

Another obstacle for socialising at work is making the time to do so. I remember the last job I had, where I was surrounded by lots of staff, and never seemed to have the time or energy to socialise. This is just part of a bigger issue of not being particularly sociable, but in essence I considered socialising with workmates a waste of my time and energy, because I already saw them at work and wouldn't have anything more to talk about. This was the wrong attitude to have, as the time spent doing something else wouldn't have been valuable for building up work relationships and potential personal relationships, which can pay dividends later on. You will know who you are more likely to get on with outside of work, and on a more selfish point, you will find out who your main threats and opportunities at work are. Who are the people more likely to become an obstacle when applying for a promotion, or help you up the career ladder? You are socialising to increase your status in the company, to learn about the hierarchy and power struggles, gain new allies, and find out who your potential enemies are.

It can be intimidating to socialise in a workmate group, especially if you are new, the group is large, and you are not the most socially adept person. But it's worth persevering with attending social work gatherings as your skills will improve in time, and the intimidation factor will diminish. Social points are, for me, one of the harder ones, because my week is currently spent being more solitary, which suits my personality, but isn't conducive to a very sociable life. I do make the effort to meet friends on a weekly basis, but it would be easier to gain social points if I worked with lots of staff.

If there are specific people who you know you don't get on with, give them a chance, because you may learn more from these people than people just like you.

Should I spend time on fringe friends?

In your social sphere, you will have people you know who aren't really close friends. They are people that you perhaps like, but haven't really bonded with enough to call close friends. I call them 'fringe friends'. These are people that you could go out with occasionally, but you wouldn't ask their advice, or have a general chitchat. For me, I find it almost impossible to spend time with fringe friends, and I use the term 'friends' loosely. This does not mean they are bad people or so removed from my personality that I don't consider them 'worthy' of being my close friends. It's just that, for whatever reason, their personalities don't quite mesh with mine. I don't spend much time with fringers because I find the experience quite shallow and unfulfilling. I like to feel that friends have some mutual appreciation of each other's company and that it is not contrived or awkward.

With fringers, the conversation is often shallow, with little depth or breadth of information exchanged. I find this a waste of my time. I'd rather build relationships with people whom I trust and admire.

Everyone you have in your social sphere should add value to your life. This can be done in many ways, but the simplest is that you like them and they make you feel nice inside when you're in contact with them. There shouldn't be any bitter 'aftertaste' once you've parted company. They have to have traits which you find fascinating and which either compliment the facets of your personality, or are similar enough for you to respect. Adding value means that they are positive, energised people, who don't drag you down or make you feel bad about yourself. You will know if they fail to meet this criteria if you question why you know this person; a thought which suggests that they are not adding value, but taking away. Neutrals are perhaps worth keeping, if they have the potential to add value in future, but don't keep them there if you are expending energy on them and getting nothing in return. These are not material things I'm referring to, but your time and effort. These resources are important, and you have to share them with people who deserve them.

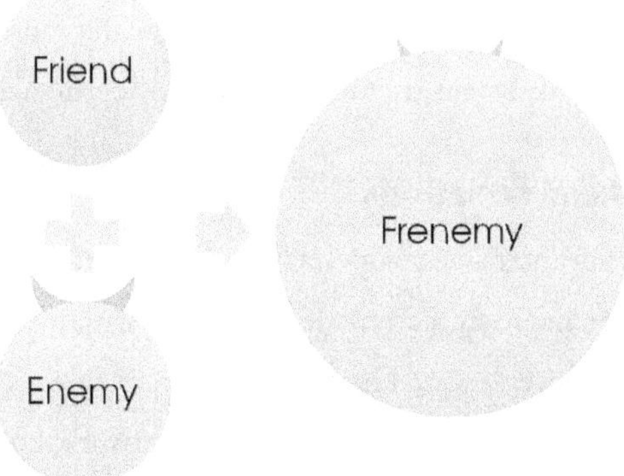

But why do so many people have acquaintances who don't really add value to their lives, and in some cases detract from it? It's quite possible that they are infected with a 'virus motive', which is a term described by Oliver James in his book *Affluenza* to imply that 'infected' people may struggle with self-esteem and other problems. The answer may lie in their fear of being alone, and insecurity in facing life as an individual rather than as a member of a social group. I'm sure it's comforting for many to feel that they have a social support network to keep them occupied. This is fine; however, considering your negative value friends – to what extent are these people actually your friends? Are you like the new Facebook generation, where it's quantity over quality? Everyone says they only have a few close friends, but that begs the question, 'why do you know so many people you don't actually like much?'

Another reason may be that you think that the more people you know the more opportunities arise for social occasions. This is a logical and useful reason to know many fringers, but again, I would argue that you must ensure that they add value to your life. Your life can be filled and surrounded by positivity, and the more people you know, the more likely you are to have people who can take that away.

Intelligent conversations

Being social means having conversations. You can't expect to meet new friends or maintain current relationships without the ability to hold a decent conversation. The level and subject of conversation will vary according to the characteristics of your network, but whatever it is, you should adapt and exude confidence in your approach. There are certain things you should consider during your conversations; tonality and body language are two important factors. I've had conversations with people who had a very monotone, droning voice, and I found it very difficult to build up any interest in what they were saying, while I find it difficult to concentrate on those with closed or awkward body language because I get the sensation that they don't want to be there or talk to me. So maintain open body language, and an engaged, varied tone.

You don't need to be a master of conversation, but if you expect people to take you seriously and respect you, you must have a wide vernacular to keep the conversation rich and intelligent. I'm sure you've had a chat with someone and within a few sentences you are made aware of how clever or not they are by their vocabulary. Body language is often deemed to be the most important factor in human interaction, with the actual words not being as important. This does not always ring true if the words being used are inappropriate, limited, and unimaginative. Then, regardless of positive body language and enticing tonality, the words can ruin the whole experience. The way I like to learn new words is by reading and using synonyms when writing as much as possible. This does not have to purvey a snobby attitude, just that you like to learn and incorporate new words into your vernacular. This is a desirable characteristic, as it shows intelligence and the capacity to learn and change. NLP is a great way of understanding body language and use of spoken words in social situations to help build rapport and trust.

A sense of humour will go a long way to help your social journey run more smoothly. If you can make people laugh then that is a bonus, because people like people who can make them laugh. You don't have to be the class joker (in which case no-one will take you seriously), but your ability to laugh and make others laugh will endear you to them and help your social sphere grow. It's fine to be serious and focused on objectives and targets, but as often as possible, try to get together with friends and have a laugh.

Social events:

Late to the party

Finding the time to meet new people is often the biggest challenge of having a busy life. I find that after I've finished work and gone to the gym, it is close to 7.30pm and my energy levels are drained. With lower energy, hunger, and time running out, it is often an uphill struggle to go out and mingle. But mingle you must.

Especially in a business context, it is common to go to networking events which go on till late. Networking events are also opportunities to meet potential friends, not just business contacts. Obviously, you will have similar concerns and interests to those who attend networking events, so that's one step closer to either a useful contact or buddy. Try to find events which tie in with your lifestyle, but you may have to make sacrifices to find the time.

I usually go to the gym Monday to Friday, but this makes it difficult for me to make evening arrangements. So every now and again I switch to just 3 or 4 sessions per week, to leave my evenings more free to socialise and network.

As with anything in life, you can find the time if you have your life under control. When people show up late for an appointment, I sometimes think 'they wouldn't be late if it was a flight they were going to'. I like the analogy; if someone is late they have not prioritised that engagement. The same can be said for any social or networking event. You have to see it as a priority, otherwise it can easily be pushed to the side and left for another day. Managing your day and meetings is a skill which you must master if you have any chance of reaching 70% – which would mean your life is rich with different activities, meetings, events, contacts, and so on, which all need to be organised appropriately. Time management requires you to know where your time is going and ensure you are allocating sufficient time to each aspect of your life so you can fit in all the things which should be done to help you reach 70%.

If you think that social events go on too late or you can't fit them into your schedule, then your mindset is not yet ready to take them on-board. This book gives you the steps and the context of each step in relation to reaching 70%, but you must get yourself in the mindset to make changes, or you'll be wasting your time.

Mix with others:

If you love it, share it

I have expressed a strong view about being discerning when it comes to your social sphere, however, as I also alluded to, it can be useful to know many people even if you're not so close. Why? Because you'll have more opportunities to share your experiences with a diverse group, rather than just a handful. This is especially useful when it comes to participating in activities you love. For example, if you sail, as I do, it's great to have a few people you can call on to join you on your adventures. This is also true for holidays. Sometimes I struggle to find people who have the time, funds, and willingness to go on the holidays I would like to go on.

You may have people in your sphere who have skills to help you build your knowledge and skills. When I first got into electronic music in my teenage years, I really wanted to learn how to DJ. At that time, there were no DJ schools I was aware of, but just by chance I met a new friend who had all the necessary DJ equipment and taught me.

Even if your friends don't have the same ambitions as you, they can offer a perspective on certain things which you never thought of before. If you have ideas, such as starting a business or developing your current business, run them by your most trusted friends and see what they think. They should give you a no-nonsense 'outsider's' opinion about your ideas, which may be more insightful than your own. Or your friends may inspire you and you'll get ideas from them. Without ideas, and more importantly, actions, we are nothing but automatons, destined to do no better than our parents and ancestors. So having an intelligent group of people you can draw ideas from and bounce ideas off is vital in keeping you motivated to achieve greater things.

By having common interests with people in your group, you can build up a network of like-minded individuals from whom you can draw energy, ideas, and inspiration. Although I have a few great friends, I often complain that I don't know enough people. This is not the fault of the world at large, but my character, which is insular and protective by nature. This is not conducive to having a large and varied social sphere, but I do try and broaden my reach whenever I can. If you have a small network, as I do, that is fine. But you must acknowledge that you will do better if you have more like-minded people in your network. I'm usually inspired by people I've never met before, such as Richard Branson, whose story urges me to work smarter and harder to achieve my life goals. But wouldn't it be better to be truly inspired and pushed by people you do know? Then you'd have a competitive reason to do better than them and, when possible, find out how they did it.

No one person can know everything, right?

You can't live in a vacuum, even if you wanted to. You could try to learn everything there is to know about everything and remain a total recluse, but you couldn't escape the need for other people. I've often thought about what it would be like to be stranded on a desert island or travelling alone in space. I used these thoughts to get me through times when people annoyed me greatly and I needed some form of mental escapism to calm me down. The reality, though, is that other people make life more interesting, not necessarily hell as Jean-Paul Sartre once wrote.

You will learn a lot from the people you meet in your life. Sometimes more so than you could ever learn from a book or seminar. This is because they are in your timeline and space and therefore their experiences have a lot to do with yours. You should pay attention to what they do right and wrong. You could go to ten self-help seminars like those presented by Tony Robbins, but I assure you, you will learn just as much from the people you know and pay a lot less. Listen to what people in your social sphere say, but also, more importantly, what they don't say. What people decide to tell you can often reveal what it is they are omitting, which is often the real essence of who they are. Also watch behaviour and actions, as they can help you improve the way you do things. Do they give sound advice or just old wives' tales? Do they often relay information they've heard or read from other people, or do they have their own informed opinions?

You can never learn everything yourself, but the more people you like and respect in your sphere, the more you can learn indirectly. Your friends will go to places you've never been and give you an honest review. They will go on a course which you hadn't thought of before. They'll go to an event you wouldn't have gone to. So friends, good friends rather than the fringe type mentioned earlier, are worth their weight in gold in terms of market research, ideas, motivation, and inspiration. You can also see the results of their endeavours, so you can judge whether you can do the same or better. For example, if one starts a new look that you didn't think would work, and it does, you can give it a try to see if it works for you. This doesn't mean you have to go around copying everything your social sphere does, but it does open your mind up to trying new things because they've already been validated by people you trust.

Family socials

Family will be part of your social sphere too, but as they are not your choice, it's quite common to have strained relationships with them. This can be due to a plethora of reasons, chief among which could be differences and incompatible personalities. You would think that if you are related you would have similar characters, but this is not always the case.

To get on with your family, there needs to be mutual care. You need to feel safe, respected, and inspired by your family.

The adage of 'you can choose your friends but you can't choose your family', implies that you are forced to like your family and remain loving and communicative even if you have nothing in common with them. Throughout my childhood, I often wondered how different I was to my parents, and family at large. My ambitions and ideas seemed part of a different world to theirs. Whenever we would congregate at family events, I didn't feel I fitted in. My parents were a mystery to me and I didn't understand a) why they were together, considering they were diametrically opposed, and b) why they decided to be parents when clearly they had no idea what they were doing. So the lesson here is: it's great if you have things in common with your family, or even if you don't, you can be tolerant towards each other.

Your childhood history, or 'the script of the family drama' as Oliver James describes in *They F*** You Up*, will greatly influence your future, but it is not unfixable if things didn't go so well. I enjoyed a fantastic childhood which deteriorated between around eight and ten years old, which is when I started to notice the negative dynamics of the family environment.

I suggest that even if you've had a turbulent childhood history, if you can forgive and forget, then do so. Keeping your family close is a nice thing, and can offer you an extra support network in conjunction with your friend network.

> ### Key point
>
> The future is malleable and you can change your mind to be positive and forward thinking. Don't let any negative family experiences control your future.

Children

Where does starting a family and having babies fit into the 70% rule? I have pondered which element to include this topic with – babies won't give you any social points until they are much older and can add LP to your life with conversation and social interaction with them and other parents. Maybe pleasure, because they will make you feel good inside and on occasion they will make you laugh and smile. Maybe they will bring you closer to your partner (if you have one), as you spend more time together and doing more activities.

Starting a family is a life choice that many people, particularly in Western society, no longer feel is necessary. More and more people are deciding not to have kids. In some European countries, such as Italy, a diminishing youth population is expounding the problem of a rising elderly population. Does this show a nation of selfish people who don't want kids for fear of losing their youth and opportunities for pleasure and freedom? Perhaps. This life is about you and your choices that both add value to your being and give you self-esteem, pride, and a moral code. Having children doesn't have to be an inevitable part of life. If kids aren't for you, rest assured that there will be others who want kids and will continue our species.

So how can having kids fit in with reaching 70%? Let's start by breaking down the various components, in an ideal situation.

- You are at a suitable age and have already established yourself in terms of reaching a base score of at least 50% in the six Life Elements; home, work, partner, social, pleasure, self-development.

- Your partner is also established with at least 50% in the six Life Elements.

- During pregnancy you will (both) learn new things about parenthood (self-development points), such as how to eat correctly, pre/post natal classes, how to feed babies, baby psychology, etc.

- During classes or appointments, you may potentially socialise with other couples.

- Pregnancy often bring families together and may allow you to socialise with family more than usual.

- Pregnancy may encourage you to take a healthier approach to living and get you exercising more, for example.

- Once the baby is born there may be a dip in physical activities but more chance to socialise with friends and family who will want to see the new family.

- Once the family settles in after a few months you may start doing more activities that are enjoyable for all involved such as walks in the parks, going swimming, and holidays.

- The child will start to bring pleasure to parents, making them laugh and smile, but remember that variety is key so they will only get 1 point, even if it happens many times per day.

- Once older, the children will be (ideally) providing you with the opportunity to gain more social and other Life Element points.

So, in conclusion, having a baby may automatically add a significant amount of points to your life, especially in the short to medium term. Although you'll love them very much, they are not given any more status than anything else (only in terms of Life Points allocation) and can limit you getting LP elsewhere, e.g. you might lose work points (maternity/paternity leave), lose self-development points (too tired to read or go to the gym), pleasure points (no more clubbing, or sex for a while), etc.

Summary

- Your social sphere is a 3D space where people can be close, distant, above and below you in a variety of different aspects.
- Practice your social skills by engaging with different types of people.
- Having a large social group is not always better but can offer more opportunities.
- Your family is part of your social sphere.
- Your children are also part of your social sphere, so bring them up well and they're likely to become your best friends.

Exercise

List all your friends and decide on those who are good for you, those who you could develop a better relationship, and those who are not really friends. Focus on the good, and ditch the bad. Also look into ways to make new friends.

> Visit 70lifepoints.com to make some new friends and share your thoughts on Chapter 9.

In the final chapter, you will get some ideas on how to put together all that you have learnt into one cohesive 'life design' whole.

Strategies and tools

As we near the end of this book, and the true beginning of your journey, let's look at some strategies and tools to help you achieve your established goals, and reach 70% on a regular basis.

"Screw it, let's do it"

Sir Richard Branson

Time management

Changing the way you live your life will largely involve managing your time effectively. There are many useful books out there that go into this in more depth, such as *Time Management* by John Adair, which I recommend you read. But to get you started, I will go through the key strategies that have helped me reach 70%.

Plan ahead

When undertaking any journey, it is wise to know where you're going, what time you need to be there, and how to get there. Your life is also a journey, and to make the changes suggested in this book, that journey needs planning. Without planning, you will be like a rudderless boat, surrounded by fog, in unknown seas, unable to make any headway towards a given destination. Go through the previous chapters to know what you need to plan for.

A large calendar/planner is a tactile way to organise your upcoming days and weeks. Put it somewhere prominent so you can't forget your tasks ahead. If you want your new routine and activities to remain private or find it more practical to have them with you at all times, then consider putting your agenda on your mobile/laptop/tablet device using an app or website. Just make sure that you have a backup or print-out of the month ahead.

Useful tools:

- A3 wall calendar
- Google calendar (sync with your mobile device)
- Task list app

I suggest you take time out every week or two (I prefer Sundays) to plan the next week or two ahead. Plan for flexibility and create redundancy; plan a bit extra in case you need to change plans, feel tired, or the event is cancelled or changed. It is not necessary to plan the whole month, as things will crop up mid-month that will provide more points than what you've planned. So you will want to take some time every Sunday to see what is coming up in the next week, then fill any gaps.

You will need to be a good organiser. This means actionable lists. By actionable, I mean tasks which are distinct and achievable. For example: 'book the spa massage for next Wednesday evening', instead of 'book a treat for myself within next few weeks'. It's easy to be swamped by lists. I have a work list which never ends. As one thing gets ticked off, another is added. But this is fine as long as you don't become overwhelmed. Sometimes I push myself too much, and I know I'm doing this when my task list requires ten people working around the clock for a week to complete. A task list of things you'll enjoy will make them easier to accomplish. Things like 'book a holiday for next weekend', is much more fun to do than 'complete my tax returns', but don't forget to allow some time to do the less interesting chores.

The key thing is to fit the activities and tasks like a jigsaw puzzle. For example, if you usually go to the gym at 7pm on Tuesday but there is a lecture that you'll find adds value to your self-development sector which is also at 7pm, you have some options:

1. Go to the gym at 5pm (assuming you can leave work early) so you'll be finished at 6pm to leave at 6.30pm, to arrive at the debate at 7pm without additional stress which could detract from the self-development points from either activity.

2. Can you objectively say that you could miss the gym on this occasion, because your regular gym attendance means youwon't lose any self-development points, and attend the debate instead?

3. Don't go to the debate because, on balance, the stress from having to rush there will detract from both activities.

4. Do a cut down gym session, skipping some elements or with increased intensity but for a shorter time, then attend the debate.

All of the above are OK, but options 1 and 4 allow you to do both activities with no extra stress – and, as you can see, require good planning and time management, demonstrating the positives of these strategies. Planning ahead is crucial to avoid making your life a hectic circus of activity with no real thought about how you expect to achieve all the things that are needed to raise your Life Score.

Prioritise

From the previous chapters, you will have already put together a list of activities that you can do realistically and which add value to various areas of your Life Elements. Some areas will need more work than others, and you may think that these are the areas that need to be worked on first. I suggest that you focus on your strengths and build a stable foundation, from which to work on the other areas that may be preventing you reaching 70%.

Hence why, with the Life Score principle, not all elements are given equal status. You have to decide which element makes up a quarter of your existence.

Your priority will be to build on the 2 foundation points of your life, so you need to plan your week accordingly. It might seem boring to focus on only two areas when you are enthusiastic for pleasure and other things. However, this is not a short-term strategy. This book is to help you prepare for the long haul. Even if your priorities change over time, you still need to focus on the present to prepare you for the future. Seeking short-term gains that are stopping you from achieving a stable platform is short-sighted and a waste of your energy. Once your two foundation Life Elements are gaining points regularly (and automatically) then you'll find it easier to gain points elsewhere.

> There have been times when I've needed discipline and a good diet to get a low enough fat percentage to see a six pack. Pretty shallow, I know, but still a thrill to see those ab lines show.

Discipline, not overwork

Discipline will be your best friend throughout this journey. Sticking with your strategy will pay off, I promise you, but you must have the discipline to continue and not be side-tracked by insignificant distractions. Your discipline in life will allow you to integrate the Life Points method with other beliefs and lifestyles, so that you know you are on the right path to fulfilment. Being disciplined also means you know how to be flexible.

But being disciplined is not the same as working yourself into the ground. Be realistic with what you can achieve in a day. If you are not being realistic, you are undermining your attempts at success, making unreachable targets, and preventing yourself achieving 70%. You can still aim high, but admit what is too high, what would overstretch you and your resources.

CBT framework

Use this structure every two weeks (I recommend a Sunday but it can any two week period you choose)

Set aside up to 30 minutes to give you time to review the past two weeks using this format:

- Events: make a note of any events/activities you did of note. Look at your calendar to remind you. For example; dinner with friends, comedy show with partner, went on date, went on holiday.

- Mood: write down how you are feeling about life in general and any specific things you feel are on your mind. Be honest about what is good and not so good. With any not so good things, make sure you balance these with positive and rational counter-comments. For example; you may write "Have been a bit anxious with work recently. My boss is giving me a hard time and I'm not being recognised for my hard work. I know that the quality of my work is of a high standard and that her opinion is not accurate. I can't expect others to see my point of view. I would prefer that my boss and I saw eye to eye, but there is no guarantee that this should be so. I can only control myself and therefore I choose to remain calm and not get stressed about this in future."

- Changes: note down any changes (both positive and negative) that have happened recently. For example, "Installed a dishwasher - I no longer have to do the dishes! I decided to break up with my partner. Have chosen a new gym and will start going next week."

- Life Points: this is where you tally up all your activities/encounters/experiences in the past two weeks, across the six Life Elements.

HOME

WORK

SOCIAL

PLEASURE

PARTNER

SELF-DEVELOPMENT

I look at my wall calendar, then use a simple counting system to add up my scores.

Your two base Life Elements (in my case home and work/social) should remain reasonably stable unless there have been significant improvements/problems/changes. Don't forget to give yourself a self-development point for doing the review!

- Homework: based on what you have reviewed, you can choose whether to give yourself homework. For example, you scored only 60 and saw that if you had been more sociable you could have reached 68. Your homework for the next two weeks could be to make an effort to be more sociable.

Visit the website 70lifepoints.com for examples of how I've added up my LP.

Your CBT style review will become a written record of your progress from now on. However, you may also want to consider putting your scores into a spreadsheet. Why? Because, if you're like me, I like numbers and graphs that can visually show me how I'm getting on.

Transport

You may be limiting your life elements because of a lack of mobility or transportation to and from any activities, e.g. the activities you like to do may not be available in the small town in which you live, but they are in the next town over. Taking the bus involves long journeys that detract from the end experience. You should consider other modes of transport; trains, car (get a license if necessary and give this self- development points), motorbike, etc. The main point is to make the journey as effortless/pleasurable/rewarding as possible, to minimise its detraction from the main event, e.g. you might cycle to an event which in itself is tiring, but is great exercise, so gives you a rewarding feeling, while still allowing you to enjoy the event. If, however, it made you so tired that you didn't enjoy the point of the journey, then you need another mode of transport.

There's so much going on, how do I know where to look?

Don't think that you have to know about everything that can be done in life. There are others who have collected that information for you. The internet is the best place to start looking for ways to improve your life. If the massive expanse of the web intimidates you, here are some ideas I have briefly mentioned before:

1. Sign up to meetup.com: this is a great place to join groups who have similar interests to you in your local area. The bonus is that because these groups can be local to you, it means you can engage with other members face-to-face, rather than remotely.

2. Groupon and similar deals websites (e.g. Wowcher, Living Social): the point with these is not so much getting a

discount, although that is an incentive to buy, but that they send you emails with ideas which you may never have thought of doing before. Every day you will have more ideas about what to do for fun, to learn, to travel, and so on.

3. Yplan: this is a mobile phone app which gives you ideas on what to do in the evenings. With these helpful apps, you don't have to think up new activities, although I would say you shouldn't rely totally on these sites – occasionally have a few unique ideas of your own!

4. A slightly more DIY approach is to look at review sites from independent reviewers, who give unbiased feedback. For example, you might not be too sure about visiting a certain city, so you could look at TripAdvisor to get some reviews from real experience.

5. Eventbrite.com

6. Theschooloflife.com

7. Oneworld.org/events

8. Lastminute.com

9. Timeout.com

10. Kweekweek.com

11. Londonist.com

12. LSE.ac.uk

If you want to attend an event on Meetup or similar, you will often be able to find reviews from previous Meetups from members, and you could email them directly to get their feedback. You don't have to jump into new things without getting some validation first. I recommend trying things regardless of mildly negative or average reviews, as long as you're comfortable with them, because sometimes one bad review can put someone off doing something that they actually would enjoy. Then, over time, you'll start to be more adventurous, and not require independent reviews.

Communicate with those around you for ideas on what you can do with your life. They may offer a unique perspective to open your mind up to new activities. Ask your friends what they do for fun, and what they'd like to do for fun. Ask your family about their activities. Even if they're not things you'd like to do, they may provide inspiration for your own idea. Meeting new people in Meetups also helps in this way. Ultimately, your aim is to fill your life with variety and positive experiences. Where these ideas come from doesn't really matter, as long as you are willing to try them. Accepting that you cannot know everything that is possible will lessen the pressure on you. Remember that you have a choice, which, as Dr William Glasser explains in *Choice Theory*, is very powerful in redefining your personal freedom.

You may think TV is a good source of such information, but I now try to avoid watching too much TV. If I counted all the hours I've spent watching TV it probably adds to years of my life in front of the idiot box. There is nothing like being able to switch your mind off after a hard day's work and vegetate in the mind-numbing content most TV programming offers. However, I would rather my mind didn't switch off so completely, and so try to do without TV during the week, or at the most watch a bit of the news.

Key point

Start to engage with the world more and you will find that you will always get new ideas. People have done the research and hard work for you.

Keeping an eye on the news not only allows you to keep abreast of what is going on in the world, but sometimes gives you useful information which you can use to expand your activities range. The added bonus of online news is being able to filter out the irrelevant stuff and focus on areas you find interesting. I tend to use the Independent or BBC News online and visit the business, technology, and science pages every day; there was an article about 3D printing which I found interesting, and I subsequently attended a Meetup group on this subject. You can use this technique to broaden your horizons.

Magazines and periodicals are a great way to keep in tune with areas that fascinate you. I subscribe to The Economist, Moneyweek, and New Scientist. These topics keep my mind stimulated with new and sometimes practically useful information. Subscribe to any publication you think will continue to give ideas. An easier alternative is to join websites dedicated to the subjects you like. E-books are also great because you can download content direct to your device, and store many books you like in the same place. I have to admit that I have so many books on my e-reader that I've left many unfinished!

Also try browsing themed websites. For science and tech, try:

- Techradar
- Io9
- New Scientist
- Science Daily

Is it worth subscribing to every newsletter?

Aside from reading the news and appropriate websites, you can also subscribe to newsletters from organisations which interest you. As mentioned, I'm interested in business, science, and technology, so I receive occasional emails from websites specialising in these subjects. This means you don't have to keep searching for new content, as it is sent to you on a regular basis.

Being interested in things keeps your mind stimulated with new content. You won't remember all of it, and you don't need to, because you will pick out the stories and information which motivate you at that time. It's a bit like advertising. Advertisers send out messages and hope that one of us will want that product at the same time the idea is planted in our mind. The same for news and information; not all of it will interest you, but occasionally some stories will resonate with you perfectly.

Being in tune with the world around you also allows you to learn what is working in the world and what isn't. The success and horror stories alike can be learning tools to help you on your path to a great life. By subscribing to a variety of newsletters, websites, blogs, groups, etc. you are giving yourself a better chance of finding new experiences and ideas, at no extra cost. Newsletters are mostly free. Most news sites are free.

Furthermore, keeping up with news (in moderation as it can also be a negative distraction) means you won't feel left behind. I'd say that not all news is useful; in fact, most of it is depressing and dull, but you can choose what you read and what comes into your inbox. Yes, by filtering, you might just miss that important insight which is the catalyst for your taking action on a certain project, but don't become obsessed with trying to have your finger on the pulse all the time. It's impossible to know everything that's going on in the world, and you don't actually want to know it all. You just want to have a fresh outlook so your world isn't a small bubble which only you inhabit. Having a wider view means you are more able to spot opportunities and value other experiences, rather than being self-centric and shallow. I've met people who have never even left the UK. I can't understand that, considering how close we are to many wonderful countries in Europe, but that is the world of many people; from their front door to work and back again.

What other ways can I be in the loop?

My concerns about Facebook aside (self-indulgence, false friendships, lack of privacy, etc.), you can use it to your advantage by joining groups which interest you and attending events. I would avoid joining groups which do not meet face-to-face on a regular basis. You don't want to become a virtual Life Junkie, but one who engages and interacts with people and things. If technology isn't your forte, don't worry, just join and check your emails every so often to see if there are any events you should attend.

There are many mobile apps you can download which can help you keep you focused on living a balanced satisfying life, such as:

- Buddify
- Lift
- Tic trac

FAQ

There are some questions or concerns that you may have about the 70% rules here, so let's take a moment to consider them.

Why are there so many rules?

I've always been fond of using step-by-step guides when learning how to do something new. If it has useful pictures, even better. Just like a flat-pack wardrobe without an instruction booklet, if you've ever read a self-help book that suggests what you should be doing to change your life but not actually how to do it, it can be frustrating.

That's why this book has clear rules; although see them as guides rather than authoritarian, because what works for me won't necessarily be the way you'd do it. Don't stray too far from them though, or you'll misjudge your points, or over/underscore yourself, which is easily done. There will be some opinion and subjectivity which crawls into each review session, but keep this to a minimum and be quite sparing with your scoring. Don't just give yourself points for the sake of it; the only person you'll be cheating is yourself, as over-scoring will give you less room to improve your life! Is that how you want to live? The more (real and earned) Life Points you get, the better you'll feel and think about yourself.

Obstacles

The necessary steps suggested in the book will be obstacles for many people. The concepts I've put forward may seem alien and bizarre to you at first, but once you overcome the barriers in your mind, you will see the bright future awaiting you. Remember that the strategy outlined in this book is the 'easy' part. The challenge will come from your mind and previous thoughts and behaviours resisting the change.

You have to believe you can incorporate the strategy I've laid down in this book into your life. Belief will get you through the times when you are not getting many points and you start to either doubt yourself, the Life Points rule, or both. Everything I've written about has worked and continues to work for me and many others. There are times when my Life Elements aren't scoring well, and I briefly question if I'm doing the right thing, but then positive actions take over and cleanses me of negative thoughts, and good thoughts and feelings come back again. These ups and downs are natural and can't be avoided, but you can certainly make sure you spend most of your time being up and that the downs aren't as low. Because the fact is, the more positive things you do in life, the more variation you have, the more control and influence on your surroundings you have, the more fulfilled and happy you'll be. I know that when I'm around 50%, I'm down, but still in a good place. Above 60% and I'm feeling good – at 70% I feel the difference and am in a great mood!

If you want the easy life, keep doing what you're doing now. Don't change, don't take actions, don't have ambition, and don't come out of your comfort zone. If change is difficult, and the end result puts you in a better position than before, then do it. Simply do it. Yes, it may be hard, but you can accomplish it, because *it has been done before*. But only you control the outcome of your life.

> ### Key Point
>
> The Life Points principle doesn't offer you a quick way out, because life isn't about quick changes. You can change your mind quickly, and take actions quickly, but long-lasting changes take time, and this is where you must persevere.

If life is a game, why take it so seriously?

You may consider life to be a game. This is an apt analogy, and in fact counting Life Points is much like a computer game, wherein the more you achieve the more points you get. However, the most significant difference from a game is that life is a one shot deal. You don't get a second chance at living this life. You will not reach the end, then be able to click a 'restart' button. Even if you believe in the claims of cryonics institutes that you can be frozen on death and resurrected at some point in the future when technology has advanced, this will not be the same life again. It will be a different version of you.

In reality, based on what we know today, your life is a once-in-a-lifetime opportunity. So why wouldn't you want to do the most with it and enjoy it? If you knew you could only do something once, wouldn't you want to get the most out of it? I know I would!

Playing any game means you are in control. If it's a board game, you roll the dice, and move your piece. If it's a PC game, you may have some spin on a character sent out to complete a mission, with you as the puppet master. You wouldn't want to play a game where you weren't in control, would you? Life is a game that you *must* win, and to do so you have to be in control. Everyone has limitations on this control, otherwise there would be anarchy, but you must control as many things about your life as possible. If you have a busy working life and a family, your life may seem out of control at times. I'm sure that, when you're getting the kids ready for school, your partner has made breakfast, and you're in a rush to beat the school-run so you won't be late for work, you must be thinking: 'this is chaos!' Whatever you can control, control, whatever you can't control, don't worry about.

What are the questions I need to ask myself?

You've gotten this far and now can start asking yourself the hard questions which will get you to 70%. Often, these answers can be hard to swallow if you've been bottling up thoughts, ideas, or emotions for a long time. The hardest thing is to ask yourself about your past. I never recommend dwelling on the past, but looking backwards at what has transpired will help you create a clearer present and future. You can avoid the mistakes and failings of the past and learn how to win. Some questions you need to think about are, 'what previous experiences have become part of my internal myth system which is potentially adding to my limiting beliefs?', 'what lessons can I learn about the past in terms of things I've enjoyed, and things that I wouldn't want to repeat?', 'are there people left over from my past now holding me back from enjoying the present?', and 'can I change the way I used to do things to try and effect a more positive outcome in the future?'

Once you've asked yourself as many questions about your past as you think are relevant to focusing on what works for you and what doesn't, then you can concentrate on questioning the present:

- Where am I now? Not just in terms of location, but your life in general
- How content am I with my six Life Elements?
- Which areas of my life need more work than others?
- Am I satisfied with any things in my life?
- What am I satisfied with?
- Are there practices I can implement today which will lead to a better future?
- Where do I see myself in two years?
- What are my long term goals?
- At what point in the future would I say I have the life I've always wanted?

Imagine where you hope to be living, and what you hope to be doing, using NLP to help visualise your future so you can also understand the steps necessary to get there.

These questions will reach deep inside of you, so you really know why you are here and what you want. This is not as easy as it sounds, because you have to be honest.

The message at the crux of this book is that you have to live your life *now*, but always have part of your mind focused on the near to medium future. Don't focus too far ahead, as this will waste your mental resources – there are too many variables and unknowns to compute. For those who have or want many interesting things in their life, life becomes at once exciting but also less predictable. This is a good thing, as long as you make sure it's an unpredictable combination of positive experiences.

Having recently come back from holiday, I noticed how tense I had been getting, and now I feel like my mind is clearer and more focused than a few weeks before.

Sifting through the mind

Many people go travelling to 'find themselves'. All this really means is getting away from the usual distractions so your mind is uncluttered and free to roam through your thoughts. You don't have to travel before you start asking questions, but it is a good idea to change the scene to encourage fresh thinking.

Do whatever you need to do, go wherever you need to go, to allow your mind some time and space to become clear. Spend a few days without checking emails (I used to be obsessed with email and check every few minutes), and if you want to go cold turkey, switch off your phone too! The aim is to have your mind clear so you can ask the questions and give open and honest answers. You don't need to know all the answers to your questions. These can be found during your quest to reach 70%. But the questions you can answer will start to give you a picture of the things you need to do and change in your life to make it satisfying and worth living.

Remain calm throughout this first process of questions and answers. You may find yourself disturbed by dredged up memories, or fears of the future, or the excitement of new challenges and the life which awaits you. Even then, you should remain calm so you are not blinded by subjectivism, nostalgia, or false hopes.

For example, basing your plans on your past experiences, emotional hang ups and desires is a simple mistake to make. This is because we all intertwine thoughts with emotions, as is human nature. But if you use emotion now to determine what you want in the future, it's likely that next week you will feel something different.

This time spent being clear and calm is critical to your success in future, because it is getting to the truth of what you are now, and what your limiting beliefs are. This will determine your path towards 70%. The truth can be made malleable, made into a new truth which is better than the old. You will soon be choosing the right percentages for your life. And although these can be amended in future, you want them to be an accurate representation of yourself right now, so you can start on the right foot and not be distracted with activities which are not really what you're about.

Isn't it too late for me?

I wish I had started my businesses fifteen years ago. I wish I had started CBT and NLP ten years ago. I wish I had started to watch my diet five years ago. All of these new things are now regular parts of my life, but I sometimes think: 'what if I had started them all sooner? I might be further along the road than I am now.' But this false thought belies an underlying hole in the logic. I probably wasn't ready all those years ago for these changes. I had many failed starts as a businessman (over ten attempts in fact!), and it took years of learning from mistakes, good practice and some luck to become successful. It's never too late to start, as the right time is *now*, not yesterday.

Your age now only reflects your experience, not your future. This you can still change, so that you can enjoy the rest of your life. As the saying goes, you are 'like a tree, and no matter how old you are, your branches extend away and bring new life'.

Say you are fifty and female. That leaves you (based on Western averages) with at least 20 more years. 20 years of enjoying your life sounds good to me! That will be more fun than most people have in their lifetimes, so don't delay in getting to 70% from today.

What are smart goals?

SMART goals are specific goals that can be measured – meaning you can track your progress, rather than just evaluating subjectively. The 'ER' of SMARTER are further additions to allow for long-term and well-measured application. The first known uses of the term occur in the November 1981 issue of *Management Review* by George Doran.

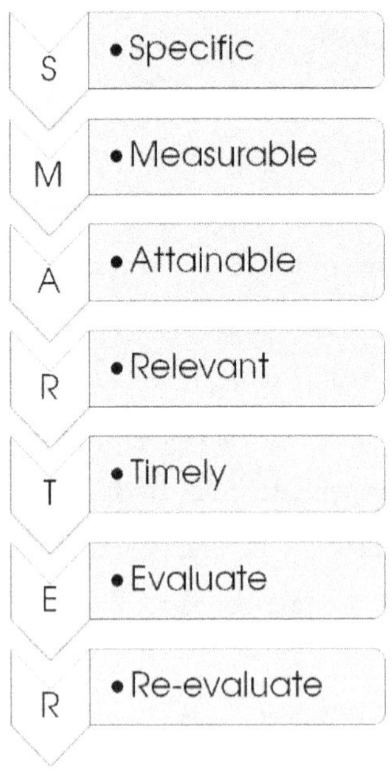

A specific goal will usually answer all of the five "W" questions:

- What: What do I want to accomplish?
- Why: Specific reasons, purpose or benefits of accomplishing the goal
- Who: Who is involved?
- Where: Identify a location
- Which: Identify requirements and constraints

By using the SMART system, in tandem with the Life Points system, you can create a blueprint for a successful, enjoyable life.

If you are not the most rational person in the world, that's OK. You don't have to be for this book. What you do need is the ability to acknowledge when you are not being rational, and have some internal mechanism to reign in any urges to act on emotional impulse. If you can't tell when you are being irrational, you will struggle to be specific about exactly what it is you want to achieve. This is because your mindset will change week on week and won't be reliable enough to keep you focused. Having goals, specific goals, is important. Specific enough to have a clear idea what results you'll be happy with, but with enough room for flexibility – without deviating too far from the initial premise of the goal. If you just say you want to win, how will you know you have won? There has to be some specific target that has been reached in order for you to know the outcome. You don't have to be too prescriptive, like 'I want to make five new friends this year', so the 6th person doesn't get a look in! Perhaps reframe this target as 'no less than four' to give yourself some breathing space.

I'm big on data. I love collecting data and compiling results to see progress. I do this for myself and my businesses and projects. If you don't collect data about yourself, you won't know if you're progressing. If you bought £20,000 in shares, I bet you would be checking on a regular basis to see if they had gone up – is your whole life not as important?

The data will come from you, be created by you, and be analysed by you, hence the need to be as objective as possible and imagine you are scoring yourself as another person. If you don't reach certain goals, that's fine. It's important you have them to give you a reason to push yourself. My overall goal, as will be yours, is to maintain 70% or more.

Ultimately, you have to set goals which are attainable – The 'A' in SMARTER. In your initial survey, you will have highlighted what you want to achieve, dismissing limiting beliefs. But there is only so much you can do, even if you push yourself to the max and fortune favours you. Set your goals big and high, but also keep an eye on reality. For example, there is no point in me deciding to become an extrovert socialite who is able to talk to women I find attractive in public, or hosting dinner parties on a weekly basis. That just isn't me. I can be that type of person for very short periods of time, but it's not sustainable. Of course, in some cases, you can have a total step change in character, beliefs, mindset, and behaviour, but in reality, try to acknowledge and build on your strengths and minimize weaknesses. Once you start to see changes, you can raise your goals to higher and more ambitious heights, but for now remain calm, and remember to be SMART.

Once you've made the decision to change, make those changes – otherwise, all the goals in the world are pointless. Then stick with those changes if they work for you. The more you follow the overall change process, the better you get at it. It also becomes a habit, and habits are easier to maintain because of familiarity of the actions and rewards (good for the process, albeit bad for individual actions). So hard work, perseverance; and eventually the habit will keep you on your path of fulfilment for the rest of your life.

Same old same old

By doing the same things you've always done, you are limiting your life to repeating past experiences. These same old experiences, however great, may be a pleasant part of your present, but progression comes from experimenting and trying new ways of doings things to improve your life.

It's a fact that, regardless of how good something makes you feel, if you always do the same things, you get bored of them.

To avoid apathy and stagnation in your life, the simple way is to add variety. Whenever I eat lobster, I make a mental note to indulge in that delicacy more often. In reality, I would probably get to about the third lobster dinner in as many days and would crave a steak! This is human nature, so don't fight it. Work it to your advantage. Stimulate your senses with new experiences. Have you ever been on a few dates and gathered that you are dating the same type of people over and over, so much so that you could barely distinguish between them? This is your comfort zone, and is severely limiting your worldview.

What if I reach 70%, and I'm still not happy?

This is a common question. The easiest answer is that if you are at 70% and you don't feel great, then you are not at 70%. You have overestimated your Life Points gained, so go back over your Life Scores and be honest with yourself about how you are scoring yourself.

So how can you know when you *are* at 70%? Einstein once said, 'compound interest is the 8th wonder of the world'. Your points system can be looked at in the same way. The more points you get, the more confidence you'll get to go and get more points. So over time, you will be doing things naturally to give yourself extra points. You will know when you are reaching 70% because you will *feel* and *think* better about yourself. It's clear that the more interesting things you do with your time, and the more you push yourself to achieve things you've never done before, the greater your overall sense of wellbeing. You will undoubtedly start to see the esoteric changes in yourself from the concrete scores you give yourself.

As your points start to amass over time, you will notice changes in your thinking. Most things you do will become measurable and repeatable ultimately building up a knowledge base of what works for and what doesn't. We need to quantify our lives to make them coherent and consistent. Mankind will eventually evolve into more rational and logic-based creatures, whereby negative emotions may well be things of the past. By looking at your life as a collection of controllable experiences, you can start to add these at your whim and create a better life. As you progress, you will remember how different things used to be, and see how much they have improved.

Your version of happiness is different to others'. I've not focused on the word 'happy' in this book for that very reason. It is too subjective. But it is a consequence of progress and getting to 70%.

Key Point

Happiness is a wonderful emotional by-product of a satisfying and balanced life.

What's the secret to keeping life consistent?

The aim is to keep your mood as high as possible while remaining in control and not letting dips last too long. There is no real secret to being satisfied all the time. Don't expect to be at 70% all the time. The aim is to be there as often as possible, and that will keep both highs and lows higher than previous periods.

Once you admit to yourself that you will go through peaks and troughs in terms of points, the pressure on trying to be happy all the time dissipates and you may find yourself being calmer as a result. When I first reached 70% I was under no illusion that this would be it for me. In fact, that is not the point. Reaching 70% is a goal, but it is a moving target. You constantly need to hit it as life changes, so you will be forever shifting and acting to hit it. This may sound daunting, as you have to remain on your toes, but it will become second nature. Understanding that you won't always get it right is a great motivator, because you won't feel pressured into constantly doing so – although this is not to say you become complacent and make it alright to have lots of peaks and troughs.

How do I find the time?

By asking yourself 'how do I find the time to do all things I need to reach 70%?' you are diverting your mind away from the real question, which is 'what am I waiting for?' You may think you do not have the time now, but will you have time in future? When exactly? There is no accurate answer unless you set aside some time to make the changes. Time management is mentioned earlier in this book, and I won't repeat those points. But what I will add is that once you've prioritised your life, and not the life controlled by others, such as family, work, friends, commitments, and so on, I assure you that you will find the time for new activities. You'll soon understand that if you don't do this, no-one will do it for you. Finding the time will eventually become easier than finding the actual Life Points to fill life with.

I try not to live by the edict that you should live everyday as if it's your last. This is a common, vague and frankly quite scary recommendation given in many a self-help book, in life coach mantras, and professed by 'guru's' at motivation speaker seminars. This way of thinking is extreme, unrealistic and puts too much pressure on you to be going at 110% all the time. I don't consider this a sustainable lifestyle. If this genuinely was my last day, I would be frantically trying to find a funeral director to freeze me and whisk me off to the U.S.A. for cryonic preservation before contacting everyone I knew and giving them some last words of wisdom! However, I do abide by the rule that you should do as much in a day, each day, as you can. Every day is precious.

The things you value, you spend time on. You know that if you dedicate time to the things you love and enjoy, you will get immediate and future rewards. The truth is that you have a filtered view of the world and have picked certain things to be regular occurrences in your life, while others, which are less favoured, have less prominence. But what if what you value is in itself stopping you from valuing other things? Have you considered that you may be spending time on the wrong values?

That is a whole other point, so for now I want to bring you back to making time for the valuable things. If you cannot find the time to do something, you don't think it is valuable enough for the time required. So you need to change your perception of it. How? Give it some time and a chance to get inside your thoughts, and see how it affects you. If it makes you feel good and positive, then it is now something worth valuing.

Other Life Junkies

Trying to improve yourself in isolation is not recommended. The very fact that you have decided to change your life dramatically for the better should be shared with as many people as possible. You will receive support and advice at times when you may get side-tracked. Becoming a member of the Life Points community at 70lifepoints.com means you are more likely to reach your goals. Just imagine yourself reaching some short-term targets which you had set out to achieve. You can share this success with others so they know what you did to get there and also give you confidence to keep going. Being part of a wider picture will provide you with a social context that this Life Points movement, the movement of becoming addicted to leading a balanced and satisfying life, is about looking after yourself but also inspiring others to do the same.

The brain works in very ancient ways, yet has evolved quite radically to deal with modern life. One aspect of human behaviour is the concept of status. This is a sense of where you are in relation to others. By being self-confident, empowered, and progressive, you are rising above the status quo where most people reside. People will see you rising above the quagmire, acknowledge that you are higher status, and aim to rise to your level. This constant shifting and progression of positive ideology will eventually lead to your social sphere being a better version of what it was before.

Ask questions whenever you are unsure about a specific element. It will take time for you to incorporate these ideas into your life, but it will happen, with perseverance. Having a mentor is a great way to make your thoughts known and get unbiased opinions, which you can heed or disregard; but at least you are gaining valuable feedback.

Is there any support available, or experts I can contact?

When you start your journey towards a 70% Life Score, you may have many questions; which you shouldn't be afraid to ask. As you continue on your journey towards a more balanced and fulfilling life, you will become more attuned to what is required of you on a weekly basis. As you become accustomed, you may find yourself asking fewer questions. This is normal, but don't stop asking questions altogether. The answers you receive may give you the insight to keep you going and fill you with fresh ideas. By joining the 70lifepoints.com website, you can find answers, while showing commitment, and that your life means everything to you. Seeking advice is natural when we need to learn. Trying to figure things out ourselves is time-consuming. Why make the same mistakes as others when they can show you the right way to do things? Replicating what has worked before is how civilisation has evolved. From mimicry comes innovation and creativity.

Mentors and 'thought leaders' are professional associates of mine whom I have chosen to provide a strong support network for everyone have gone through and continue to enhance their lives with the Life Points system. These experienced thought leaders are on hand to guide you through the steps necessary to attain 70% and fulfilment. Once you join the website, you will be assigned a thought leader or mentor depending on your membership level, with whom you discuss your progress on a regular basis.

Once you have been through the Life Points process and followed it meticulously, you can also teach others to do the same.

You will be proof that the Life Points system works. This may lead to you becoming an ambassador for Life Points, recommending this book to your friends, so they too can start living, and giving you more of a sense of achievement and satisfaction. Once all your friends are doing it, their friends will do it too and, before you know it, your local community, and wider, will be in better moods, more positive, more aware of themselves and their potential. This 'flooding' of positivity can start from *you*! If I inspire just one person to take control of their lives, stop making excuses as to why their lives are crap, and use my ideas and systems to regularly reach 70%, my work is done.

Can I just wing it without keeping track of everything I do?

Did you ever have a diary as a kid?

I had a Tony the Tiger diary (the protagonist from the UK cereal Frosties). I remember being so thrilled about writing about me, and having a record of my thoughts and actions. The habit of writing daily didn't last very long though. As with most things, I got bored of it, and stopped after a month or so.

Since then, I haven't kept a record of my thoughts, but imagine if I had. I'd have a vast amount of data about myself from which I could learn. Instead, I have to rely on memory, which gets distorted, rearranged, and forgotten over time. Since doing my fortnightly Life Points review, I now have a record of my journey. Its main intention is not to be a diary as such, but a way to offload thoughts which are clogging my mind, assess my performance, and set myself homework if need be. With the addition of the Life Points system, I now also have a numerical and objective record of my actions since the inception of measuring my Life Score. This has been put into a spreadsheet so I can see what I'm doing right and where I need to improve.

By logging your progress you too can build up an objectified picture of your life. If you are not technical (which you don't have to be), then simply write your thoughts and scores down.

By visualising your progress, your mind makes real your initial concepts of improvement or failings. There is no doubt that a powerful image tells more than just words or sounds. I remember going to the dentist recently. While having my teeth checked, the dentist said, "You don't floss, do you?" I replied, "I used to, but I can't be bothered. It's too time-consuming and uncomfortable." As I said that, she maneuvered the monitor screen in my direction and asked me to watch a short animation about the dangers of gum disease. It showed how without flossing, the gums become inflamed, and bleed when touched, and eventually, the gums start to recede, revealing more tooth until they fall out. Pretty grim viewing, but it worked– I now floss every evening! Imagery can motivate you to push on and improve. If you see you are being more sociable on the graphs described, when before you spent more time alone, then that will show you can do it and encourage you further. Much like stock markets, the numbers tell one story but it's really the graphs traders want to see – the trends visualised.

When will my life be balanced and satisfying?

You should not live for a future time when you will be fulfilled and happy. The point is to enjoy *today* and plan things for tomorrow which will enhance your life even further. Keep an eye on the future, yes, but live in the moment and appreciate what you have now. By regular practice, you are more likely to reach your 70% goal sooner, and maintain that score over the long term. You can never say when you will be happy, but by setting targets and putting plans in place, I can say for sure that you *will* reach that point.

You are heading towards a brighter and more rewarding future. You must believe this and put doubts about your ability to succeed away – your success relies on your self-belief. Sometimes you will not believe it or will feel that life is unfair when others are leading (in your opinion) better lives. These are the times when the brain will come to your rescue. When you make changes to your thought process, over time your brain starts to reshape and 'rewire' its activity, as proven with neuroplasticity, which suggests that as we fire more neurons towards the same synapses, the path become more 'trodden' and therefore easier to cross next time. This is the essence of learning. By taking the steps described in this book, you are learning and eventually will make a habit of success.

Being impatient about when you will achieve 70% will hinder your progress. It's too easy to say to yourself that things are not working, rather than that things are working but slowly. Look at the big picture: your life as a whole. Will the content of your life be great memories, or painful regret? It will be a combination of both, but your aim is to ensure that you spend as much of it as possibly in the 70% zone. On the graphs described above, there will be ups and downs, but you will be able to spot an overall upward trend from a distance. Regardless of how much time you spent below 70%, you are heading towards it now, and will reach it sometime soon.

CONCLUSION

Well done for making it to the end of this book.

By now, you will have taken yourself through a journey of self-discovery to find out exactly what you want and need in your life to make it balanced and satisfying.

Here is a summary of what you have learnt:

- Your life is made up of six Life Elements (in no particular order):

  1. HOME: The place and area in which you live
  2. WORK: The regular activity that consumes your time and energy during working hours
  3. SOCIAL: The people in your social sphere such as friends, acquaintances, and family
  4. PARTNER: Any person you are intimate with
  5. SELF-DEVELOPMENT: The practice of bettering yourself in a variety of ways
  6. PLEASURE: Activities which stimulate your mind and body and make you feel good

- You decide on the maximum points available for each

element, based on your priorities at this time.

- A Life Point is given for each aspect and activity you do in each of the Life Elements.

- You will try to get as many points as possible for each element, as counted every two weeks.

- Your aim is to reach a total of 70 Life Points every two weeks. This is when you will feel that your life is satisfying and balanced.

- Once you know how to get to 70 points, you will try to regularly achieve this Life Score.

- Every two weeks, you will count your Life Score and make notes on what you did well and, if necessary, areas for improvement.

I wish you the best, and if you'd like some support, then contact us at the 70lifepoints.com website.

RECOMMENDED READING

Chapter 1: What is happiness?

Ferris, T. (2011) *The 4-hour work week*, London: Vermilion.

Frankl, V. E. (2004) *Man's search for meaning*, London: Ebury.

Levitin, D. (2008) *This is your brain on music*, London: Atlantic Books.

Maslow, A. H. (July 1943) *A theory of human motivation*, Psychological Review, Vol 50(4), p 370-396.

Mill J. S., *Autobiography in The Harvard Classics*, Vol. 25, Charles Eliot Norton, ed. (New York: P. F. Collier & Son Company, 1909 (p. 94), or page 100 in columbia university press 1960.

Rand, A. (1964) *The virtue of selfishness*, New York: Signet.

Chapter 2: What is stopping you having a great life?

Doidge, N. (2008) *The brain that changes itself*, London: Penguin.

Heffernan, M. (2012) *Wilful blindness*, London: Simon and Schuster.

Kelsey, R. (2011) *What's stopping you?*, Chicester: Capstone.

Peck, M. S. (1997) *The road less traveled and beyond*, New York: Simon and Schuster.

Rand, A. (1963) *For the new intellectual*, New York: Signet. Smart, J. (2013) *Clarity*, Chicester: Capstone.

Chapter 3: The 70% Life Points strategy

Rath, T. (2007) *Strengths Finder 2.0*, New York: Gallup Press.

Chapter 4: Self-development

Glasser, W. (1985) *Positive Addiction*, New York: Harper colophon.

Lawless, J. (2012) *Taming tigers*, London: Virgin Books.

Rhinehart, L. (2010) *Book of est*, Raleigh: Lulu.

Chapter 5: Home

Lyubomirsky, S. (2010) *The how of happiness*, London: Piatkus.

Chapter 6: Work

Bernstein, A. (2010) *The myth of stress*, London: Piatkus.

Pink, D. H. (2008) *A whole new mind*, London: Marshall Cavendish International.

Pink, D. H. (2010) *Drive*, Edinburgh: Canongate Books.

Rand, A. (1999) *Atlas Shrugged*, Reprint edition, New York: Plume.

Reed, J. and Stoltz, P. G. (2011) *Put your mindset to work*, London: Portfolio Penguin.

Chapter 7: Partner

Gray, J. (2012) *Men are from Mars, women are from Venus*, London: HarperElement.

Kahneman, D. (2012) *Thinking, fast and slow*, New York: Farrar, Straus and Giroux

Klinenberg, E. (2013) *Going solo*, London: Duckworth Overlook.

Ross, L. (2011) *The secrets to sensational foreplay*, Berverly: Quiver.

Rufus, A. (2003) *Party of one: The loners manifesto*, New York: Marlow & Company.

Chapter 8: Pleasure

Burns, D. (2000) *Feeling Good*, London: HarperCollins. Dawkins, R. (2007) *The God Delusion*, London: Black Swan.

Jeffers, S. (2007) *Feel the Fear and Do It Anyway*, 20th anniversary edition, London: Vermilion.

Pert, C. B. (1999) *Molecules of Emotion*, London: Pocket Books.

Peters, S. (2012) *The Chimp Paradox*, London: Vermilion.

Sandel, M. J. (2013) *What Money can't Buy*, London: Penguin.

Skidelsky, R. and Skidelsky, E. (2013) *How Much is Enough?*, London: Penguin.

Chapter 9: Social

James, O. (2007) *Affluenza*, London: Vermilion.

James, O. (2007) *They f*** you up*, London: Bloomsbury.

Chapter 10: Strategies

Adair, J. (2009) *Effective time management: How to save time and spend it wisely*, Revised edition, London: Pan Books.

Glasser, W. (1999) *Choice Theory: A New Psychology of Personal Freedom*, London: Harper Perennial.

FAQ

Doran, George T. *There's a S.M.A.R.T. way to write management's goals and objectives*. Management Review 70.11 (Nov. 1981): 35.